The Arcado-Cyprian Dialect

Herbert Weir Smyth

[Extract from *Transactions of the American Philological Association* for 1887, Vol. XVIII.]

J. D. L. Lyon

Cambridge

V. — The Arcado-Cyprian Dialect.

BY HERBERT WEIR SMYTH, PH.D.,

JOHNS HOPKINS UNIVERSITY, BALTIMORE, MD.

RECENT investigations in the field of Greek dialectology have chosen to restrict the term "Aeolic" to the dialect of Lesbos and of the adjacent mainland. Formerly "Aeolic" referred with more or less fluctuating usage to Lesbian, Thessalian, Boeotian, Elean, Arcadian, and Cyprian. This delimitation of "Aeolic" is the result of that revolution in the study of the Hellenic dialects which has broken definitely with the old-time division of Strabo, a division which now finds its sole support in the authority of the name of Curtius. (See Windisch, Georg Curtius, eine Characteristik, p. 13 ; Curtius, Kleine Schriften, II, 150–163.) In place of the ancient and revered, quadrilateral division, there has now been substituted that into $\bar{a}$ and η dialects.[1] The cause of the adoption of a new terminology is at once apparent if we consider that Strabo's "Aeolic" is made to comprise each and every peculiarity of speech that is not Doric or Ionic-Attic.

In the paper published in the American Journal of Philology, 1887, Vol. VII, 421–445, I attempted an examination of the interrelations of the dialects of Thessaly, Boeotia, Lesbos and Elis, and sought to portray their connection with the North Greek of Locris and Phocis. It is the purpose of the present article to submit to a preliminary examination the last member of the so-called Aeolic group — the Arcadian dialect — in the hope of defining its interrelations with other Hellenic dialects with greater precision than has hitherto been done. The material here collected is designed to serve as the basis of a discussion of the question in a volume on the Greek dialects now in preparation.

---

[1] Cf., for example, Pezzi, *La Grecità non ionica nelle iscrizioni più antiche* in the Memorie della Reale Academia delle Scienze di Torino, 1883, pp. 251, 252.

Boston
1888.

As any examination of the morphological and syntactical features of Arcadian cannot be complete without reference to those of allied dialects, it is imperative in the first instance to draw within our horizon that dialect with which Arcadian is in keenest sympathy. It has therefore been my aim to examine every word-form in the inscriptions (as also many of the Hesychian glosses) in the light of the agreement or difference of Arcadian and Cyprian; to offer new or modified explanations of individual forms when this seemed necessary; and to illustrate the phenomena of dialect life in Arcadia and in Cyprus by constant reference to similar or divergent phenomena in all the other Hellenic dialects. It is singular that so important a period of the life of the Greek language as the Arcado-Cyprian dialect has never been reconstructed in its entirety so far as the paucity of materials at our command permits any such reconstruction. If attained, it presents a wide outlook over the early history and configuration of the dialects.

The dialect of Arcadia was discussed for the first time in a separate paper by Gelbke in the second volume of Curtius' Studien (1869). This treatise is not thorough, and its explanation of points of detail, is, as a rule, antiquated. In the tenth volume of the Studien (1878), Schrader undertook to separate the "Aeolic" from the Doric features of Arcadian. The course of the following investigation will show that Schrader's manipulation of material is not happy; and his paper does not deserve the praise bestowed upon it by Wilkens in his discussion of the Greek dialects in the ninth edition of the Encyclopaedia Britannica. Finally Spitzer, Lautlehre des Arkadischen (1883), has offered a most valuable contribution to the subject by submitting to an elaborate investigation certain portions of the morphology of the dialect. It is to be regretted that this treatise, though disfigured here and there by incautious conjectures, did not extend its horizon so as to embrace an examination of all the phenomena which go to make up the Arcadian dialect.

As to Cyprian, I have had to base my results upon my own studies of the inscriptions of Deecke's *corpus* in Collitz's

Sammlung, Vol. I, and of those that have since come to light,[1] so far as they have come to my knowledge. Rothe has submitted to a partial examination the vowel relations of the Hesychian glosses (Quaestiones de Cypriorum dialecto et vetere et recentiore, Part I, 1875). Both this treatise and that by Beaudouin (Étude du dialecte Chypriote moderne et médiéval, 1884) leave much to be desired. In the American Journal of Philology, Vol. VIII, 467–471, I have made a list of words generally regarded as poetical, but found in Cyprian prose. Greek dialectologists cannot fail to welcome so indispensable an auxiliary to their investigations as the promised grammar of Cyprian forms by Dr. I. H. Hall. That part of Meister's second volume which deals with Arcadian and Cyprian, though printed has not appeared. While the present sketch of Cyprian chiefly deals with but one source of information concerning the dialect, — the epigraphic material, — it is hoped that it may serve not merely as a comparison between Arcadian and Cyprian, but also as a preliminary summary of the grammar of the latter dialect.

My plan in detail embraces an attempt at establishing the character of the Arcado-Cyprian dialect, *i.e.* of Arcadian before Cyprian attained to the dignity of individual existence. This is undertaken in two ways: (1) By tracing all those points of agreement which are the exclusive property of Arcado-Cyprian. (2) By collecting all those instances of phonetic and inflectional resemblance which are the joint property of both Arcadian and Cyprian and of other Hellenic dialects.

It is apparent that the first category is of incomparably greater importance in determining the character of the primitive Arcado-Cyprian. It is no new observation in Greek dialectology that phenomena which are exclusively confined to one dialect are extremely rare. Their very rarity enhances their value. The singular sympathy of the Hellenic

---

[1] Pamphylian forms have occasionally been drawn into discussion when they seem in close touch with Cyprian. But cases of agreement between Arcadian and Pamphylian alone have been left unnoticed, *e.g.* Ἐχλας, Pamph. Ϝεχέτω. A Boeotian Ϝεχλας does not exist.

dialects with each other, despite the configuration of Hellas, voices itself in the fact that one dialect is differentiated from another by displaying merely more or less allegiance to another dialect, be it that of a neighboring or even of a distant speech-centre. Qualitative distinctions here often resolve themselves upon nearer view into quantitative differences. In discussing the instances of joint similarity, I have endeavored to distinguish, as far as possible, the age of the phonetic change in question, since chronological distinctions, oftentimes overlooked in dialect investigations, are of an importance that can scarcely be exaggerated. Those phonetic changes that occur in a period of declining dialect vigor are manifestly of little importance for the establishing of a prehistoric dialect. For example, to the overreaching character of the Â declension, the -ες declension has yielded, after a stubborn resistance, many of its most characteristic forms.

Then as to the points of divergence, which are oftentimes as powerful factors in determining the position of a dialect as the points of contact. It has been my aim to register each case in which Cyprian has followed a different phonetic path from Arcadian ; and when Cyprian — or, *vice versa*, Arcadian — does not offer as yet an example of the phenomenon in question, care has been taken to allude to this fact to prevent the possibility of erroneous conclusions being drawn from the unjust application of the argument from silence.

Besides the necessity of noting whenever Arcadian or Cyprian corresponds with Doric or Ionic, or with both, it was imperative to discover in the dialects of the "Aeolic" type (*i.e.* Lesbian, Thessalian, Boeotian, Elean) their points of agreement with Arcadian or with Cyprian. Hence I have arranged the Arcadisms not found in Cyprus under the following heads : *Arcadian and Aeolic, Arcadian and Thessalian, Arcadian and Boeotian*, etc. ; and wherever two or more of these dialects are in agreement I have essayed, as far as was in my power, to bring them into line. The same course has been held with Cyprian, that it might be brought into the clearest focus.

Phonetic changes common, for example, to Arcadian and

Boeotian, and which reappear in Doric alone, are placed almost invariably under the head of *Arcadian and Boeotian*, from a pardonable desire to throw the strongest light upon the points of contact between Arcadian and all the dialects tinged with "Aeolism." But by this convenient principle of division it is hoped no prejudice will be excited against the possibility that the form in question is not Doric in character. It is not my purpose, nor is it in my power, to answer all the vexatious questions that start up from every side, the deeper one penetrates into the many-colored phenomena of the dialect life of Hellas. But when it seems tolerably clear that we have to deal with a loan form (though I am by no means certain that I have always made a decision which is satisfactory even to myself), I have preferred to group this class under a special head. Though for my immediate purpose the most coherent principle of division seems to be that of the various dialects of the "Aeolic" type in their connection with Arcadian or with Cyprian, I am conscious that this point of departure, rather than that of phonetic changes, has brought with it a certain incoherence, for which the index may be at least a partial remedy.

The points of agreement and difference between Arcadian, Cyprian, and other dialects having been exhausted, I have given a list of the chief specific peculiarities of the two dialects under discussion.

The tie which bound metropolis and colony is nowhere more strikingly indicated than in the domain of language. Thus, for example, we have τόνς τάνς in Argos and in Crete, the infinitive ending -μειν, possibly a contamination of -μεν with -ειν, in Rhodes, Agrigentum, and Gela. And in fact throughout the entire history of Greek colonization the colony clung with an affection to the language of its source which ever awakens the sympathies of the philologist — Sparta and Heraclea, Thera and Cyrene, Megara and Byzantium, Corinth and Corcyra, etc.

Without any express testimony on the subject, we might with safety conclude upon an examination of the epigraphic material that Cyprian stood in nearest touch with the parent

Arcadian. But in this case the evidence of language is un-equivocally supported by the testimony of antiquity. The Arcadian descent of the original Greek settlers of Cyprus is asserted by Paus. VIII. 5, 2: ' Ἀγαπήνωρ δὲ ὁ Ἀγκαίου ἐς Τροίαν ἡγήσατο Ἀρκάσιν. Ἰλίου δὲ ἁλούσης . . . χειμὼν Ἀγα-πήνορα καὶ τὸ Ἀρκάδων ναυτικὸν κατήνεγκεν ἐς Κύπρον καὶ Πάφου τε Ἀγαπήνωρ ἐγένετο οἰκιστής. Cf. also Herodotus VII, 90, Strabo XIV, p. 684, and the conjecture given below on page 124.

The connection between Arcadian and Cyprian is perhaps closer than that between any other dialects of Hellas, that have at the same time such varied points of divergence. If we consider the very early date of the settlement of Cyprus by Arcadians, the long years of total separation afterwards, we cannot fail to account the close touch between Arca-dian and Cyprian a most remarkable fact. The settlement was made in all probability before the Arcadian settlers in Cyprus had made to any great degree practical use of the Greek alphabet. It seems scarcely credible that a Greek alphabet of any developed character, and in constant use, should have been completely displaced by the Cyprian syl-labary, though commercial intercourse with the Phoenicians was frequent from at least 1100 B.C. Yet it cannot be too distinctly asserted that writing became known to the early Peloponnesians through the intermediation of the Achaeans and Ionians, and that it was known in the Homeric age even if it is not alluded to in the Iliad and Odyssey. This is clear from the character of the alphabet in Thera, Melos, and Crete, as well as in Lycia and Phrygia. The suppression of a Greek alphabet in Cyprus is a fact noteworthy for its very isolation. See Wilamowitz, Hom. Untersuch., p. 290.

SPECIFIC PECULIARITIES OF ARCADO-CYPRIAN.

The following points of contact date from the Arcado-Cyprian period, and are shared in by no other Hellenic dialect.

1. -αυ in the genitive sing. masculine Â declension. *Arcadian:* Ἀγαθίαυ, 1231, B 38; Ἀλεξιάδαυ, 1231, B 25; Γοργιππίδαυ, 1231,

B 37; ἐργωνίαν, 1222₄₂; ϝιστίαν, 1203₁₈; Καλλίαν, 1231, B 19; cf. C 49; Φιλαίαν, 1189, A 75; Φιλλίαν, 1231, B 17; and in thirty-two other words in Collitz's Dialekt-Inschriften Sammlung (C D I), with seven cases of -αν, the former part of the word having been lost. *Cyprian:* Ἀρισταγόραν, 28; Ἀριστίγαν, 20; Ἀτίταν or Ἀτί(ν)ταν, 25; Θεμίαν, 66; Ἰαρώ(ν)δαν, 118; Μαράκαν, 29; Νασιώταν, 21; Ὀνασαγόραν, 60₁.₂,₂₂; Στασίγαν, 17; for Ταμιγόραν, Hall, Rev. Journal A. O. S., XI, 233,[1] read Τιμαγόραν; Ὀνασιμάλα[υ], C D I, 120; Ὀνασαγόραν Τιμογόραν, Berl. Phil. Wochens., 1886, pp. 1291, 1292, 1612; Πυνταγόραν, ibid., 1612.

The quantity of α in -αν is uncertain. Brugmann, Gramm., § 79, suggests ᾱυ; G. Meyer, ᾰυ. If short, ᾰυ from ᾱυ, when standing originally before an initial sibilant of the following word (twice before a consonant, four times before a vowel in the inscriptions) might be explained as Ζεύς from *Ζηυς, νᾶυσί from νᾱυσί. But we have here rather a lightening of the masc. case termination in the Â decl., appearing also in πολίτου; which is not from analogy to ἀνθρώπου, but from *πολιτηο, whence πολίτεω and *πολιτεο. See Bechtel in Bezzenberger's Beiträge X, 283.

The converse of this contraction of αο to αυ is seen in the Ionic Καοκασίων ταοτα, etc. The υ of Arcado-Cyprian αυ is not *ü*, but the old *u* sound. We must distinguish sharply the dialectic change of final and of medial αο, since in Boeotian medial αο alone became αυ; in Arcado-Cyprian medial αο never contracts to αυ. Τ[ρ]αύχαε, Roehl, 127, *i.e.* Coll. 871, and Σαυκράτεις, Σαύμειλος, which are adduced by Blass, Aussprache,[2] p. 63, G. Meyer, Gramm.², § 120, as examples of α + ο = αυ, admit of another but not certain explanation,[2] which may also hold good in the case of the forms in Λαυ- (*e.g.* Λαυδικεύς in late Attic). On the Arcadian fem. gen. in αυ, see p. 103.

NOTE. — The more original form -αο (as in Homer and in Boeotian) is found in Cyprian, but never in Arcadian. But two forms occur: Δαγατίσαο (or Δαῖτίσαο), 58, and Κυπραγόριο, 79, both of uncertain date. In order to escape from the necessity of regarding this -αο as a survival of the original -αο, an assumption which excites the hostility of surprise if in Arcado-Cyprian final αο became αυ, it is advisable that we regard this -αο as due to the orthographical fluctuation between αο and αυ. Such variation is, it is true, chiefly Ionic, but found also in Attic: Αὐτοκρά[τ]ης; Kumanudes, Ἀττ. ἐπιγρ ἐπιτ., 2597. It is difficult to see whence Cyprian -αο could have been borrowed, as

[1] This inscription is regarded as spurious by Voigt and Deecke.

[2] By parallelism of the forms of the base σαϝο-, viz. (1) σαυο-, σαο-, and (2) σαυ before consonants, σα- before vowels. (See Spitzer, Lautlehre des Arkadischen, pp. 43, 44.)

ao had ceased to exist except in Boeotian at the period in which these two inscriptions were composed; and that -ao should have become -av both in Cyprian and Arcadian, after their separation, is improbable. If the above explanation, which I present with hesitation, be not adopted, another possibility will the more readily gain the suffrage of scholars, — that the Cyprian forms in -ao are nothing more than conscious archaisms.

2. ἀπύ with the dative.[1] *Arcadian :* ἀπυέσ[θ]ω δὲ ὁ ἀδικήμενος τὸν ἀδικέντα ἰν ἀμέραις τρισὶ ἀπὺ τᾶι ἀν τὸ ἀδίκημα γένητοι, 1222 3-5. *Cyprian :* ἀπὺ τᾶι ζᾶι τᾶι βασιλῆϝος, 60 8, 17; ἀφ᾽ ὧι ϝοι τᾶς εὐχωλᾶς ἐπέτυχε, 59 3 (*a · po · i · vo . i*).

In No. 103 Deecke reads [ἀ]π᾽ ὠτοδακῶ(ν), but *po ·*, which is written cursively by Deecke should rather be upright, as it is uncertain; and *ta ·*, upright in Deecke, ought to be cursive. Hall has *ko ·* (or *po ·*) *i · to · ta · ko ·* (or *po ·*).[2]

3. ἐς, *i.e.* ἐκ ἐξ with the dative. *Arcadian :* Κύριοι ἐόντω οἱ ἐσδοτῆρες τὸμ μὲν ἐργάταν ἐσδέλλοντες ἐς τοῖ ἔργοι, τὸν δὲ ἐργώναν ζαμιόντες ἰν ἐπίκρισιγ, 1222 49-50. *Cyprian :* ἐξ τῶι ϝοίκωι τῶι βασιλῆϝος κὰς ἐξ τᾶι πτόλιγι, 60 5, 6; ἐξ τῶι χώρωι τῶιδε, 60 11; ἐξ τᾶι ζᾶι τᾶιδε ἰ ἐξ τῶι κάπωι, 60 24. Cf. p. 72 for Cyp. ἐσς.

4. νσι in the third plural active. Doric, Elean, North Greek, -ντι; Boeot., -νθι; Aeolic, -ισι.[3] *Arcadian :* κ[ρ]ίνωνσι, 1222 5; κελεύωνσι, 1222 15; παρετάξωνσι, 1222 28 (from παρετάζω in the sense of ἐξετάζω). *Cyprian :* ἔξο(ν)σι (*e · ke · so · si ·*), 60 31, where Deecke transcribes ἔξωσι. In the same line ἴωνσι (*i · o · si*) ; but as Deecke has ἴωσι, this case of similarity between Arcadian and Cyprian is not free from suspicion.[4]

The Pamphylian dialect, though in its ground-type Doric in character, is so frequently colored by its proximity to Cyprus, that its forms may here be offered in evidence, *e.g.* ἐξάγωδι, 1267 16. Here we have δι = Doric τι, but no ν graphically expressed, though it was the cause of τ becoming δ.

It cannot be shown that the -νθι of Boeotian and (probably) of Thessalian is the middle sound between -ντι and -νσι, or that it is anything more than a local affection. The assibilation in Aeolic and Arcado-Cyprian has no need to seek its cause in Ionic influence.

---

[1] M. Geyer, Observationes epigraphicae de praepositionum graecarum forma et usu. Altenburg, 1880, p. 25.

[2] Meister in the Berl. Phil. Wochens., 1885, p. 1604, reads πολ τῶτακῶ.

[3] Cf. Müller, De Σ littera inter vocales posita, p. 70.

[4] Brand, De dialectis Aeolicis, p. 22, writes -νσ·; so also Johansson in Nägra ord om dialekter, p. 31.

5. πός = *Arcadian :* πός, 1222₅₄ ; ποσκατυβλάψη, 1222₃₃ ; πόσοδομ, 1222₉. *Cyprian :* πός, 60₁₉₋₂₀, ₂₁ ; and perhaps in ποεχόμενον, 60₁₉, ₂₁, if Deecke is correct (Collitz Sammlung, I, p. 12). Meister, however (Berl. Phil. Wochens., 1885, p. 1604), claims that this ποεχόμενον represents ποιεχόμενον, and finds ποῖ in ποῖ τώτακῶ, Coll. No. 103 (the accent is uncertain : ποῖ or ποί). At present ποῖ has turned up in the Oeanthean inscription, Coll. No. 1479₁₅ (about 430 B.C.) [1] ; in Troezen Cauer,[2] 62₉ ; in Epidaurus, Ἐφημ. ἀρχαιολ. 1883, p. 211, l. 2 ; cf. Et. Mag. 678₄₄, ποῖ παρὰ Ἀργείοις, and Steph. Byzanz. *s. v.* Ἁλιεῖς ; in Boeotian, Ποίδικος, Coll. 553₁₃ ; in the Delphian month Ποιτρόπιος, Cauer,[2] 219₃ ; and finally in Corcyraean, ποῖ τὸμ, C. I. G. 1838 a 3, ποῖ ταί, C. I. G. 1840₁₇, though Blass (B. B. XII, 193, 196) writes πο<τ>. Arcado-Cyprian πός is not formed from *ποσί<ποτί, nor does it stand in any conceivable relation to περτί, πορτί, προτί, or πρός, as is held by Meister, I, 44, Brand, De dialectis Aeolicis, p. 54. Nor is there any trace of the existence of a pan-Doric or pan-Aeolic *prti, which has been regarded as the fruitful source of all these various forms. In the Berl. Phil. Wochens., 1885, p. 1604 (cf. Baunack, Inschrift von Gortyn, p. 22, note), Meister adopts the following explanation of the descent of πός and ποῖ : —

$$\text{ποτί}$$

A.-C. ποσί* before cons.   A.-C. πός before vowels.

This presupposes the retiring of *ποσί in Arcadian after the separation of Cyprian, and the origin of ποῖ from *ποσί. Only under this supposition could ποῖ have become πό in ποεχόμενον. This explanation is radically defective : first, because *ποσί, like the Pelasgians, is there only to be driven away ; and secondly, because it ignores the correspondence between ποῖ and Lettic *pĭ*, Lithuanic *pi*. Bechtel (B. B. X, 287) has clearly pointed out that πός is for ποτ + ς (cf. λελυκός < −οτ + ς), whether ς was directly affixed to πότ or to ποτί. Italian dialects fall easily into line with *obs*, *sus*, Oscan *puz*, etc. This explanation is preferable to that of Johannson (Några ord om dialekter, p. 32, note), whereby πός = ποτί before a vowel ; to that of Prellwitz, which compares directly *pos-t*, *pos-sideo*, Lithuanic *pas ;* and to the equation of Spitzer, ἐπί : ἐπ :: *ποσί : πός. As a

[1] πό adduced as Locrian (cf. Allen, Curt. Stud., III, 271) is now read ποτούς, Coll. 1478₃₃, for πὸτ τούς.

matter of fact, ποῖ is generally used before a consonant, πότ before vowels (Baunack, Studien, I, 12; Prellwitz, G. G. A. 1887, p. 439).

In Coll. 68 we have ποτ', an inscription which shows the influence of the epic verse, according to Deecke. See, however, Hall, A. O. S. XI, 220. It is possible that a ποτ(ί) may be due to an imitation of the epic dialect, which has ποτί, but only in composition. I prefer, however, to read ποτ(ε) with Allen, *Versification*, p. 150. In the same line we have πότι, which is supposed by Spitzer, p. 47, to be the result of an unfortunate attempt to give an epic coloring to the Cyprian πόσι. πότις for πόσις is not Greek, the IE suffix *ti* becoming σι generally in Doric, and Homeric φά-τις μάν-τις are but indifferent analogues. It cannot be doubtful but that πόσις was the genuine Cyprian form, as the dialect shows no little hostility to τι; cf. σίς, σί βόλε, etc.

The preferences of the different dialects may here be given: Aeolic, πρός and πρές (?); Thessal., ποτί and πότ; Boeot., ποτί and προτί; Pamphyl., περτί.

NOTE.— The parallelism which has been assumed on account of a supposed genitive in -ων in the O declension in both dialects is unwarrantable. In Cyprian, cases of -ων are not infrequent ('Οναίων, 21, Berl. Phil. Wochens., 1886, p. 1290; Νωμηνίων, *ll.* 1886, p. 1323; Θεοτίμων, 42; 'Αβιδμίλκων, 59; πε(μ)φαμέρων, 59; Φιλοκύπρων, 60₁; 'Ονασικύπρων, 60₂₋₃,₁₁,₃₀; 'Ονασίλων, 60₂₄; ἀργύρων, 60₇,₂₅₋₂₆; ταλά(ν)των, 60₇; ὑχήρων, 60₅,₁₅ (not ὑχῆρων as Deecke), Δρυμίων 60₁₉. The Arcadian τωνί, in agreement with τῶ ἐπιζαμίω, 1222₃₆, is not τω-νί (= τουτουί), but τω-νί, νι having been taken from τον-ί(δ), ταν-ίδ, etc. Cf. δι from τοδ-ί, ταν[ν]ί 1222₅₃, and the Thessalian particle -νε in τοῦν-νε-ουν 345₁₇ equivalent to Homeric and Aeolic -δε in τοῖσ-δε-σσι, τῶν-δε-ων. See Baunack Studien, I, pp. 55, 56. The ν of the Cyprian genitive singular is as yet unexplained, though perhaps it may be regarded as a relic of this -νι or νε,[1] which may have attached itself to the pronominal declension in Cyprian; cf. μέν for μέ in κά μεν ἔστασαν, 71,[2] and μι in No. I, which may either represent με or μι(ν).[3] This suggestion is certainly nearer the truth than that of Ahrens (Philologus, 1876, pp. 12–13). Ahrens assumed an older ending -ως, which from the analogy of -μεν -μες, αὖθιν αὖθις, etc., became -ων. Another explana-

[1] Since writing this I learn that Bezzenberger has already made the same conjecture (G. G. A., 1887, p. 427). Cf. the change of -δι to -δε through influence of δέ.

[2] Cf. ἐμίν = ἐμέ, Kaibel, 322 (214 A.D.), Sardis, probably a slip. The Tamassus inscription (Berl. Phil. Wochens., 1886, p. 1323) has τόν(ν)υ according to Sayce, which is adopted by Deecke. The stone has, however, according to Pierides, *to· ne.*

[3] μιν occurs in 45 according to Voigt and Hall. Read μι(ν) εὐξάμενος περὶ παιδὶ τῶι Περσεύται μιν ἔθηκε ἱ(ν) τύχαι. Certainly no meaning can be extracted for ὐ in ὐ-ευξάμενος.

tion — by analogy of the plural -ων — has only slight support, the singular generally exercising a controlling influence upon the plural, as ἡμεῖο upon ἡμείων.   As regards the explanation from -νε -νι suggested above, care must be taken to distinguish this -ν from the ν ἐφελκυστικόν, which is entirely absent from Cyprian (see on p. 110), as it is from Aeolic, Thessalian, and [1] Boeotian non-κοινή prose inscriptions; in Arcadian it is of extremely rare occurrence.

The points of contact between Arcadian and Cyprian, which are the possession of these two dialects and of none other, are, it is true, but few.   Their important character, however, embracing both phonetical and syntactical correspondences justly entitles them to claim a unique position in stamping the relation of these allied dialects.   The comparatively isolated position of both dialects, their hostility in these instances to the ingression of Greek forms of another type, have here served to shelter memorials of a prehistoric age.

Extending our range of observation by a gradual widening of our horizon, it will first be necessary to notice two features in which Arcado-Cyprian is in touch with Homeric usage alone.

ARCADO-CYPRIAN AND HOMER.

1. Infinitive termination -ηναι.   *Arcadian:* κατυφρονῆναι, 1222₄₇; ἀπειθῆναι, 1222₄₆.[2]   *Cyprian:* κυμερῆναι, 68₄, is preferable to Ahrens' κυμέρναι; cf. δοϝεναι, 60₅,₁₅, of uncertain accent.   Outside of Arcado-Cyprian this termination occurs in Homer and nowhere else.   Fick (Ilias, p. 395) refers the Homeric form φορῆναι in B 107, H 149, to a Cyprian source.   The same form, K 270, rests, according to this scholar, upon imitation of the poem B–H, which he thinks was composed either by a Cyprian bard or for a Cyprian audience (Ilias, pp. 258–259, 394).   For a brief statement of the grounds of this theory, see A. J. P., Vol. VIII, 479–481.

On the origin of the form, see Spitzer, p. 45, who supposes that ἀπειθῆναι is either from *ἀπείθημι or from *ἀπειθέγεν with assimilation to the -ναι inf. ending.   The treatise of Johansson (De derivatis verbis contractis) has put the -ηναι forms in a totally different light.

---

[1] Thessalian seems often to have had recourse to a ν which is not ν ἐφελκ. e.g. -ν in the infinitive ὀνγράψειν, δεδόσθειν.

[2] ἦναι is from *ἔσ-ναι, as ἠμί<ἐσμί, by combination of Doric η and Ionic -ναι. See page 94, note 1.

2. *Arcadian:* βολόμενον, 1222 ₂₄. *Cyprian:* σί βόλε· τί θέλεις,
Hesychius. Cf. βόλομαι in Homer, Λ 319, a 234. The Aeolic βόλ-
λομαι, Doric, Pamphylian [1] βώλομαι (Boeot. βωλά), Thessalian βέλλειται and Εὐβολῖνος, Boeotian βείλομαι, may have a different present
stem from that contained in the simpler Arcado-Cyprian form. Thus
βολ- may, through βολνο or βολιο, have been the progenitor of βολλ-,
etc. The possibility of reduction of the double liquid even in prose
cannot, however, be gainsaid. All the above-mentioned dialects,
however, agree in having the original β sound before the obscure
vowel sound o, the Locrian, Delphic δείλομαι, the Heraclean δήλομαι,
having the dental representation of the palatal *g* before the clear
vowel ε.

Arcado-Cyprian and Aeolic.

Strong stem κρετες- for the later and weaker κρατες-. *Arcadian*
(in Tegea and Kletor): Αὐτοκρέτ[ης], 1246, D 17; Καλλικρέτης,
1246, B 15 and B 3 (gen.); Σωκρέτης, 1231, C 1; Τιμοκρέτης, 1231,
C 50 and -(τε)ος C 23, 1246, C 9; Εὐρυκρέτης, 1231, B 32; Νεοκρέτεος,
1189, A 61 (not Μενο-); Πολυκρέτεια, 1237; Εὐθυκρέτης, Le Bas-
Foucart, 338 b₃₂. *Cyprian:* Ἀριστοκρέτης, 71; Τιμοκρέτης (?), 121;
Τιμοκρέτεος Φιλοκρέτεος, Berl. Phil. Wochenschr., 1886, pp. 1290, 1291;
-κρέτης, 148.

κρέτος is called Aeolic by Joh. Gramm. 244; ἐπικρέτει, Alc. 81, by
emendation; cf. Alc. 25. κρέτος, according to Buttmann's conjecture in the scholiast on Vespae, 1234.

These dialects also possess forms from the base -κρατες-, which,
morphologically speaking, is later than -κρετες-. *Arcadian:* Ἀλεξι-
κράτης, 1181, B 29; Ἀριστοκράτει[α], 1238; Ἀριστοκράτης, 1181,
A 12; Ἀστυκράτης, 1211 ₈,₅; Δαμοκράτης, 1249 ₈; Δαμοκρατίδας, 1181,
A 5; Δεξικράτης, 123 Γ, C 36; Ἐπικράτεος, 1204, -εος, 1204; Εὐκρά-
της, 1248₄; Καλλικρατίδας, 1239; Κρατέαυ, 1240₅; Νεοκράτη[ς],
1246, D 16; Νι(κο)κράτεος, 1189, A 36; Ξενοκράτεος, 1248₅; Σωσι-
κράτης, 1231, C 49; Τιμοκράτης, 1181, B 11; [Φ]ιλ[οκ]ράτεος, 1246,
B 11. *Cyprian:* Στασικράτης, 17, -εος, 18; Κυπροκράτιϝος, 2. Thessalian and Boeotian have -κρατος, never -κρετος.

Since the weak base -κρᾰτες- appears as early as Homer, it is probable that both forms existed side by side in Arcado-Cyprian, the
κράτος type (from nom. κρέτος, gen. *κϝτέος), not having been able

---

[1] ἐβωλάσετυ, 1267₈; βωλήμενυς, 1267₁₃; not βολ-, as is read by Brand De dialectis Aeolicis, p. 22.

to completely displace the other.   Other examples of a supposed
pan-Aeolic ερ for αρ are θέρσος, Aeolic ἔρσην, ἱερός, βέρεθρον, Arcad.
Ἐρίων, etc.   Cf. p. 90.

ARCADO-CYPRIAN AND THESSALIAN.

Arcadian : πτόλις found only in Pausan. VIII. 12. 7 : καλεῖται δὲ
τὸ χωρίον τοῦτο ἐφ' ἡμῶν Πτόλις.   If this evidence be accepted
together with the testimony of the inscriptions, Arcadian had both
πτόλις and πόλις.   But the epigraphic monuments have only the
latter form, which is also Aeolic, Boeotian, Elean, Pamphylian, Doric,
and Ionic.   *Cyprian :* πτόλις, 60. Cf. Schol. Ψ₁, πτόλιν] πόλιν. Κυπ-
ρίων τῶν ἐν Σαλαμῖνι ἡ λέξις.   Cyprian has no case of πόλις.   *Thessalian :* οἱ ττολίαρχοι, 1330 ; ἀρχιττολιαρχέντος, 1330₂ ; from οἱ πτολ-,
which is a change of medial, not of initial, ππ to ττ ; cf. Λεττίναιος
and Brugmann, Grundriss, §§ 333, 654₄.   πόλις also occurs in
Larissaean inscriptions.

It is difficult to make this word any dividing line between the dialects without including the other case of ππ < π + parasitic ι, *i.e.*
πτόλεμος, which is Homeric, Attic, and Cyprian, according to Hera-
cleides in Eustathius, 842, 62 ; and πτόλεμος occurs on a Cretan
inscription, C. I. G. 2554₁₉₇.   It seems, therefore, that the other
dialects never developed the ππ- form of these words.

There is no firm link connecting Arcado-Cyprian with
Thessalian which does not at the same time serve to connect
either Aeolic or Boeotian.

ARCADO-CYPRIAN, AEOLIC, THESSALIAN.

1. The preposition ἀπύ = ἀπό.
Arcadian : 1222₃, ₄, ₁₃, ₃₅, etc. *Cyprian :* ἀπὺ τᾶι ζᾶι, 60₈, ₁₇. *Aeolic :*
Sappho, 44 ; C D. I., 213₁₅ ; 238₁₀, etc. *Thessalian :* 345₈, ₂₃, 1308.
2. *Arcadian :* κέ (in conjunction with ἄν), 1222₂.[1] *Cyprian :* κέ
in ἤ κε (= Attic ἐάν), 60₁₀, ₂₃, and in ὅπισίς κε (= ὅστις ἄν), 60₂₉.
Cyprian has κέ alone, never ἄν. κέ is also *Aeolic* and *Thessalian ;*
κέν is Aeolic and Homeric alone. κά is the form of this particle in
Doric, North Greek, Boeotian, and Elean.

---

[1] This is disputed by Kirchhoff Mon. Ber. Acad. Berl. 1870, p. 52. Arcadian
is the only dialect except the Homeric that possesses both κέ and ἄν. Boeot.
κάν, 488₃₆, a document composed in Attic, is καὶ + ἐάν. ἄν occurs seventeen
times in 1222; ἄγ, 1227₅.

NOTE. — The impossibility of explaining ἡ in ἦ κε as the exact phonetic equivalent of εἰ (despite Deecke's statement in B. B. VI. 79, that η in ϝήπω is regularly used for εἰ) has lead G. Meyer, Gramm.,² § 113, to regard ἦ κε aὶ ἦ(ν) κε = ἐάν κε.   On this supposition, which is apparently adopted by Fick, Odyssee, p. 324, Arcadian and Cyprian would stand on a plane in possessing both ἄν and κε.   That we are not driven to assume a Cyprian ἤν is, however, clear from the fact that ἡ and εἰ may in reality be different case forms of the stem sve/₀. Baunack, Inschrift von Gortyn, p. 50, suggests that αἰ is the locative of the feminine svā-, ἡ the instrumental, and εἰ the locative of sve/₀-. The Heraclean Tables have fifteen cases of αἰ, one of ἡ (I, 77), and one of εἰ (I, 127).   The latter may be due to κοινή influence, which is not infrequent in these Tables.   Other examples of ἡ are C. I. G. 2483, 2484, where διαψαφίξα-σθαι ἡ δοκεῖ (cf. Ahrens, II, 381), and in the Gortyn inscription, IV, 31, ἡ δέ κ' ἀποθάνῃ τις; cf. V, 9, ἦ κ' ἀπ(ο)θάνῃ ἀνὴρ ἢ γυνά, αἰ μέν κ' ῇ τέκνα, etc.

This explanation solves the difficulty of the interrelation of ἡ (Cyprian), αἰ (Homeric, Aeolic, Thessalian, Elean, Doric, and Boeotian (ῇ)), and εἰ (Ionic, Attic, late Doric, and Arcadian[1]).   Cyprian ἡ cannot be either the ancestor or the descendant of αἰ or of εἰ.

ARCADO-CYPRIAN, BOEOTIAN, THESSALIAN.

1. Treatment of the preposition ἐκ ἐξ.[2]

Arcadian: ἐς, 1222₄₉, before a consonant; ἐσδέλλοντες, 1222₄₉, and the following forms before a consonant in 1222: ἐσδοθέντων, l. ₇; ἐσδοθῇ, ₅₂; ἐσδοκαῖς, ₅₁; ἐσδοκαῦ, ₄₀; ἐσδόσεσι, ₁₆; ἐσδοτῆρες, 6, 15, 18, 48; ἔστεισιν, ₃₇.   ἐξ occurs in ἐξέστω, 1222₂₁; Ἐξ(ά)κεος, 1203₃; Ἐξακί-δαν, 1204; and ἐγ in ἐγγόνοις, 1233₆,₇.[3] *Cyprian:* ἔξβασιν, 32 (Deecke), where ξ represents σσ (e·xe·pa·si·ne·); ξ before β is, however, contrary to Greek phonetics, wherefore M. Schmidt transcribes ἔσς-βασιν. ἐς τῶι ϝοίκωι, 60₅₋₆; ἐς τᾶι πτόλιγι, 60₆, etc. Curtius wrote ἔσϲονσι, Kleine Schriften, II, 105.   *Boeotian:* ἐς before vowels, e.g. ἐς, 571 a 4 App., 713 b 8; ἐσσεγράφε[ι], 735 (ἐξ, 400 a 4 App., 712₂; ἐξεῖμεν, 497₉; and frequently elsewhere).   ἐς before consonants in composition, e.g. ἐσγόνως about 25 times; cf. ἐσκηδεκάτη, 951₂ (but ἐξ, 502₄; ἐξεί[κον]τα, 502₁₂).   ἐκ is also Boeotian, 383₂; cf. ἐγγόνοις, 493₈.   *Thessalian:* ἐς, 1329, I A 15, before a consonant and in com-position, as ἐσγόνοις, 345₁₉; ἐσδόμεν, 345₂₀; ἐσθέμεν, 345₄₂.   Before a

[1] In 1222 and in no other Arcadian inscription.

[2] On this, see Curtius, Zu den Auslautsgesetzen des Griech. Kleine Schriften, II, 104.

[3] Collitz (Verwantschaftsverhältnisse, p. 8) is not strictly correct in referring ἐσγονοι to Arcadian.

vowel we have no case of ἐos; cf. ἐξεργασθείσεσθειν, 345₁₇,[1] and ἔξ, 326₁; ἐξείκοντα, 326₄. ἐκ does not appear in any document composed in pure dialect. ἐξ in Thessalian and Boeotian is certainly, and in Arcadian and Cyprian probably, due to κοινή influence. ἐs *cum gen.* before consonants, ἐξ before vowels, is also Cretan.

2. Extremely problematical is the assertion of Spitzer (Lautlehre des Arkadischen, p. 23 ff.), that in Arcado-Cyprian final ᾱι, ηι, ωι became ᾱ, η, ω, and that, while the other dialects accepted this change at a comparatively late date, Thessalian and Boeotian suffered the same loss of the final ι at a period when Cyprian had not been differentiated from Arcadian.

The grounds for this hypothesis are as follows : In Thessalian and Boeotian ει from ηι arose, not from the loss of one mora of the ē sound, but through η. It will, however, be noticed that ει may have come from ηι at a time when ει had already become ῑ. ου from ωι in Thessalian and in Boeotian arose from ω, and not from οι. οι is then, according to Spitzer, a pure locative, and had nothing to do with ωι originally.

Now, as to the facts in Arcadian and Cyprian, Spitzer asserts that both dialects possessed the dative ωι and the locative οι. In Arcadian we have no example whatsoever of -ωι, -οι occurring in πολυμήλο[ι, 1200 = Roberts, 277 ; ἡμίσσοι, 1222₂₅; αὐτοῖ, 1222₁₂, 1233₂,₆; ἔργοι, 1222₃,₄₉,₅₄. -οι is the form which has either partially or entirely displaced the dative -ωι in Arcadian, North Greek, Boeotian,[2] late Elean, and Eretrian. In Cyprian we find -ωι, -ω, and -οι, according to Deecke. (1) -ωι : ϝοίκωι 60₆ ; Ἀβροθάωι (?), 129, 130 ; μισαάτωι, 126 ; οἶϝωι, 60₁₄ ; Ὀνασίλωι five times in 60 ; τῶι fifteen times in all ; τῶιδε, 60₁₁,₂₄ ; θιῶι, 37, 61, 66(?), 75(?) ; δεξίωι, 37 ; ἤρωι, 41, 96(?) ; Ἀμύκλωι or -οῖ, 59₈. (2) -ω : ϝ' Ὠρω, 41 ; Μαγιρίω, 120 ; τῶ about sixteen times. (3) -οι : μυχοῖ, 85, is doubtful, according to Deecke (Hall has μυχοῖα) ; Παφοῖ, 56 (Hall, Πάφοι, voc.) ; Ἠδαλιοῖ, 62.

To maintain his theory, Spitzer demands that every case of -ωι should be expelled ; and Cauer, in the Wochens. für kl. Philologie, 1884, p. 99, asserts the correctness of -οι over against Deecke's -ωι.[3] But even Ahrens (Philologus, XXXV, 13) upholds the datives in -ωι and -ω parallel to the locatives in -οι. The burden of proof rests

---

[1] Perhaps influenced by ἐξεργαθήσεσθαι of Philip's letter in κοινή, which immediately precedes.

[2] It is not necessary to agree to Brand's assumption that before the separation of the various "Aeolic" tribes, the locative was used for the dative.

[3] In his *Delectus*[2] (1883) he wrote ϙ.

clearly on the shoulders of those who maintain that both old case forms do not exist contemporaneously in Cyprian ; nor should the loss of ⸗ωι in Arcadian prejudice the case against its occurrence in Cyprian.

As regards ηι both dialects are in agreement. The final vowel is lost, the η never shortened. *Arcadian* has, in 1222, τυγχάνη, ἔχη, and ποσκατυβλάψη. *Cyprian* has συλήσῃ, 126 ; Ἄδη, 126 ; ὀρύξῃ, 60 12, 24, 25 ; λύσῃ, 60 29. The only case of ηι is Ὕϝηι, 124, which is not very certain. The age of all these inscriptions is such that any theory as to the loss of final ι from ηι in Arcado-Cyprian times builds upon a perilous foundation. The age of Alexander the Great witnessed the breaking down of the ι ἀνεκφώνητον.

Finally as to αι : Spitzer claims that Arcadian αι is not ᾱι (either from ᾱ + αι, *i.e.* dative, or from ᾱ + ι, *i.e.* locative), but is from analogy to οι, and is the representative of the locative ; while ᾱ is from ᾱι, and represents the dative. The latter form was, however, lost. In Cyprian, on the other hand, ᾱ may be the representative of the old dative (ᾱ + αι) or of the old locative (ᾱ + ι). Cyprian αι is of the same origin as Arcadian αι. According to the common transcription we read in Arcadian τᾱι, 1222 54, as a relative, 1222 41 ; in Cyprian, ἀρούραι, 60 20 ; μάχαι, 60 3 ; ἀζαθᾱι, 3 f. ; τᾱι eleven times, τᾱιδε, 60 14 ; τᾱ at least four times. As the form stands, ται may be a pure dative, >ᾱ + αι ; cf. Mahlow, Die Langen Vocale, A. E. O., p. 53. Or the αι may be a locative, if pan-Hellenic ᾱι>ᾱ + ι became ἄι. Upon the question whether ᾱ + ι became pan-Hellenic ἄι or pan-Hellenic ᾱι, and whether -αι is from analogy to -οι or is an I.E. case-ending[1] with atonic α, as in νύμφᾰ, depends the character of the Arcado-Cyprian forms. It is not possible, from the limited material at our command, to determine whether Arcado-Cyprian αι is ᾱι or ἄι.[2]

In view, however, of the uncertainty attendant upon this problem, and of the possibility that Thessalian and Boeotian ει and ου may not be authoritative for the period of the coexistence of Arcadian and Cyprian, it is advisable at present to leave the question to a more thoroughgoing investigation.

ARCADO-CYPRIAN, AEOLIC, THESSALIAN, BOEOTIAN.

There is no single morphological or phonetic feature shared in alike by each and all of these dialects to the exclusion of

[1] See Brugmann, Gramm., § 82.

[2] Brand, De dialectis Aeolicis, p. 47, holds that ἄι is the Arcadian form.

all others.   Nor is there any dialectic peculiarity of authoritative certainty connecting them all together by the operation of one and the same law.

1. Not beyond peradventure is the assumption that the older pronunciation of v as I.E. u, and not as $ü$ (introduced in Asiatic Ionic and Attic not before the fifth century?), survived in these dialects as well as in Pamphylian, in Chalcidian, and in the Laconian vulgar dialect.[1] M. Schmidt (in K. Z., IX, 366), Ahrens (in Philologus, XXXV, 8–9), Blass (Aussprache,[2] 35), have assumed the u pronunciation for Cyprus.   Fick (Ilias, p. 256) claims on the strength of Ἀμόντας (Coll. 147) and the Hesychian glosses quoted, p. 76, that the Cyprian v had a leaning towards o, *i.e.* the closed o, which makes against the $ü$ sound.   This means of representing the v sound is found in Boeotian (Ἀμόντας, 603; ὀπερδικιόνθω, 429₅), late Laconian (κονοουρέων, C. I. G. 1347₉, for κυνοσουρέων), dialects which had the u sound.[2]   For Aeolic, cf. Priscian I, 27.   Spitzer, p. 18, claims that this was the Arcadian as well as the Cyprian pronunciation.   The relation of v to o is, however, the sole basis for this assertion, as it is in the case of Aeolic.[8] The Boeotian pronunciation is certain from the use of ov for v (at first for $ū$, later for $ŭ$).   Thessalian ov for $ω$ seems to point to $ü$, Νυμεινίοι, 345₂₅ >νεϝομήν(ν)ιος being but an indifferent foundation for Prellwitz's attempt (de dialecto Thessalica, p. 13) to overthrow the conclusions of Blass, Aussprache,[2] p. 36, which are supported by Cauer, Wochens. für kl. Philologie, 1886, No. 33.[4]

This supposed connecting link between Arcado-Cyprian, Aeolic, Thessalian, and Boeotian, has been referred to here, since much has been made of it, especially by Curtius, Kleine Schriften, II, 160–162, as a means of demonstrating the original close relationship between all these dialects.   As a matter of fact, even if in all these dialects v was pronounced u, nothing would be proved thereby as to their inter-

[1] The literary monuments and inscriptions of Sparta have no trace of ov for v, hence Blass assumes that the pronunciation of the cultivated classes may have been $ü$.   Other traces of u are Corinthian Ϙυλοίδας, Roehl, 20₄₇, and Chalcidian Ϙύϙνος, C. I. G. 7611.

[2] Ὄλομπος, C. I. G. 8412, an apparently Ionic inscription, and Cretan Πότιος, Rangabé, 2478, I, 23, are doubtful.

[8] Wilamowitz (Hom. Untersuch. 288) maintains that the pronunciation as u was retained till the time of Pindar, and that Aeolic, Cyprian, and Eubaean Ionic (in the modern Kuma and Stura) had the old u.

[4] Brugmann, Grundriss, § 48, excludes Thessalian from the list.

connection, since they would have only preserved for a longer period than other dialects a common heirloom such as ᾱ, ϝ, etc. Only if it can be shown on other cogent grounds that Lesbians, Thessalians, Boeotians, and Arcado-Cyprians were once united as a distinct tribe or ethnic unit, is this assumed retention of the I.E. sound *u* to be regarded in the light of corroborative evidence.

2. Change of o to υ.

Closely connected with the retention of I.E. *u*, is the change of o to υ, which is heralded as one of the most salient features distinguishing alike all these dialects.

Arcadian : ἀπύ six times in 1222, both separately and in composition; ἄλλυ, 1222₃₈ (cf. δεῦρυ, Herodian II, 933₉, but δεῦρο, Sappho, 84) ; κατύ<*κατό, as a direct change of α to υ, is impossible.[1] κατό is from analogy to ἀπό: cf. Elean ὑπαδυγίοις from analogy to μετά, etc. κατύ occurs alone 1222₁₁,₂₉, and in composition ποσκατυβλάψη, 1222₃₈ ; κατυστάση, 1222₄₃ ; κατυφρονῆναι, 1222₄₇. It is so far attested in Tegean alone. Finally, -āo becomes -αυ (or -ᾱυ) in the genitive.

Cyprian : εὐϝρητάσατυ, 60₄ ; ἐϝρητάσατυ, 60₁₄ ; γένοιτυ, 60₂₉ ; ὡρίσετο, 126 ;[2] ὐν- for ὀν = ἀνά in ὐνέθηκε, 45 ; but only if we adopt Deecke's reading in preference to that of Voigt and Hall (μιν ἔθηκε), which to my thinking is superior. ὀνέθηκε occurs about six times, and ἀνέθηκε twice. Finally, in -αυ<-āo as in Arcadian. The manifest fondness for υ of Cyprian is supposed to be attested furthermore by the Hesychian glosses in which υ is held to have passed into o : μοχοῖ· ἐντός (in No. 85 Deecke reads μυχοῖ; Hall, μυχοῖα) ; ἰνκαφότευσε· ἐγκαταφύτευσε ; θόρανδις· τὸ ἔξω. But other dialects made use of o instead of ου to represent the I.E. *ŭ* sound, *e.g.* Boeotian,[3] late-Laconian. Cf. also ὀγρός in Syra, θομός (for *ū*) in Crete.

Pamphylian : ἐβωλάσετυ, ὐ βωλήμεννς, Ἐστϝέδινς, Ὑδραμούαυ, Ηιαρῦ. The Pamphylian examples can scarcely be due to Doric influence in view of the vicinity of Cyprus.

Aeolic : ἀπύ, 213₁₅, 214₄₅, 238₁₀, 250₁₄, 232₈, 248₈,₉, 311₂₄,₂₉ (the only epigraphic examples of the change), Sappho, 44, 78. The κοινή ἀπό appears, *e.g.* 281ₐ,₂₂,₃₄,₃₆ ; ὑμοίως, 271ₐ,₆ ; ὕσδος, Sappho, 4

---

[1] Aeolic σύρκες (gramm.) is but an apparent exception; <*σόρκες?

[2] Spitzer claims (p. 17) that the Arcadian forms were -τυ and -ντυ. This is by no means certain, though we have no example of -το or of -ντο.

[3] Ἀμόντας, 603, as in Cyprian Ἀμό(ν)τα, 147. Fick, Ilias, p. 256, ventures to explain Κοπρῆος, Ο 639 as due to the Cyprian o for υ.

(perhaps); ὑμάρτη, στύμα, ὕμοιος, ὑμάλικες, Theocritus.   All other examples are doubtful.

Thessalian: ἀπύ, 345 3, 23.

Boeotian: Δέρμυι, Δέρμυς, 875, Δαμόθοιννς, 689, are quoted by Pezzi (La Grecità, etc., p. 260), as possible examples of the substitution of υ for o before 403 B.C.   The latter example is now read by Meister, -θοιν[o]ς or -θοιν[ί]ς.   Boeotian is confessedly the weakest member of the group, but Herculean efforts have been made to wheel into line this, according to Boeckh, the oldest of the "Aeolic" dialects : —

ἀπό is explained as being practically equivalent to ἀπύ or ἀπού; and Διουκλεῖς, Νιουμών, [Θ]ιουτίμυ, are cited as having ου = υ = o. On the other hand, o stands for υ in ὁπερδικιόνθω, 429 ; cf. οὑπερδικιόνθω, 430.

ἀπύ is certainly a striking joint possession of Arcado-Cyprian, Aeolic, and Thessalian.   Boeotian, Elean,[1] and Pamphylian, alone stand out against a pan-Aeolic ἀπύ, which is the only word that even the most determined advocate of the prehistoric interconnection of these dialects can claim as pan-Aeolic.

If *non res ipsa sed frequentia exemplorum* as regards υ for o be held to be a peculiarity of "Aeolic," it cannot be denied that at least four of the above dialects show a tendency which on any fair view must be held to date so far back as to point to some sort of closer connection.   In Ionic examples of υ for o are rare ; but in Doric they are more numerous, though at best sporadic.   Cf. G. Meyer, Gramm.², § 62.

It is pretty clear that of the two short o sounds, one became closed at a very early period in Greek.   The second o of ὄνομα must have suffered this change to a partial extent before the separation into dialects.   In other words, the closing of the open o came later, but certainly in Arcado-Cyprian, Aeolic, Thessalian, and perhaps Boeotian, at a period before a similar tendency came into existence in Doric and Ionic.

NOTE 1. — Cyprian Πρυτίτω, 149, is perhaps connected with πρό as πρύτανις and possibly πρύμνα and πρυλέες.   The Aeolic form is, however, πρότανις.

NOTE 2. — It is singular that in a dialect with so pronounced a predilection for υ as the Arcadian we should nevertheless have ὄνομα.   In Arcado-Cyprian the substitution of υ seems to be confined to the final syllable of words having more than one syllable.   An A-C ὀν = ἀνά is therefore very doubtful.

[1] Roehl, 556, has ὑνέθηκε.   G. Meyer suggests that the inscription is Laconian rather than Elean.   But neither Laconian nor Elean has any example of the "darkening" of o.

There is no link between Arcado-Cyprian and Boeotian which does not at the same time serve to connect Arcado-Cyprian and Thessalian or Aeolic.

The vigorous preferences of Arcado-Cyprian for the dialects of the Aeolic type alone having thus been disposed of, it is now imperative to again widen our circle of observation. The keener our hunt after traces of kinship between Arcado-Cyprian and other dialects, the more urgent is the necessity of beholding its ever-enlarging sympathies. Nor is this necessity obviated by our feeling that, in proportion as we enlarge these dialectal circles, the phenomena in question lose in authoritativeness. In estimating the propensions of a dialect, the course of investigation shows that a slight touch is oftentimes more indicative of genuine or, it may be, of original sympathies than rude masses of color. A qualitative, not a quantitative, standard can be of value here. The circles in question grow in extent till the last embraces those phenomena which are obviously, if not actually, pan-Hellenic. As before hinted at, it is here that it is oftentimes difficult to determine whether we are dealing with a pre-dialectal survival of Hellenic speech, or with a formation that is merely incidental to an early innovatory stage of the period of actual dialectal existence.

Arcado-Cyprian and Ionic.

The infinitive termination -ναι referred to above, p. 69.

Arcado-Cyprian, Aeolic, Ionic.

τι = σι in the terminations of the verb (-οντι, -ωντι) are treated differently as regards the preceding vowel, but all agree in the assibilation. On Cyprian ἴω(ν)σι or ἴωσι, see p. 66. Doric, -οντι, -ωντι.

Arcado-Cyprian, Doric, Ionic.

Nominative in -ης from η stems. The η declension parallel to that in ᾱ has survived in a few sporadic examples in Greek. Its existence in Latin, in the so-called fifth declension, substantiates the belief that in Greek it antedates the separation into dialects.

Arcadian: ἱερής, 1231, B 34, C _{1, 29, 30}; ἱαρής, 1235; γραφής, 1230₇, 1236. *Cyprian:* ἰγερής, 33, is the only example, the common form in ευς being found in No. 40. βασιλεύς is frequent in Cyprian, and there is no example of βασιλής. Arcadian has neither form. Outside of Arcado-Cyprian the η inflection has generally been displaced by that in ηυ, as in Aeolic. The following examples, however, occur: Homer, Ἄρην; Archilochus, 48, Ἄρεω < Ἄρηο; cf. Ἀντιφά-την, ο 242, by the side of Ἀντιφατῆα, κ 114. Ionic ἱέρεω, Olbia, C. I. G. 2058, A 23; Tomoi, Arch-epigr. Mitth. VI, 8, No. 14.[1] Doric Τύδης, Ὄρφης, Φύλης; cf. Lat. *Ulixes Achilles.* G. Meyer is incorrect when he attempts to explain ἱερής for ἱερεύς from analogy to εὐγενής, since the genitive of ἱερην- is in its oldest form ἱερῆϝος, to which εὐγενέος offers no parallel. Cf. G. Meyer, Gramm.², §§ 323, 324; Bechtel, Inschrift aus Eresos, in the Göttingen Nachrichten for June 30, 1886; Spitzer, Lautlehre des Arkad. p. 27; Johansson, De verbis derivatis contractis, p. 74. The Boeotian forms in -ει = η (Εἰρωίλλει, Μέννει, Φίλλει, etc.) are doubtful. It was suggested by me (Der Diphthong EI, p. 41) that they were survivals of the η declension, an explanation adopted by Bechtel, p. 378. Others regard them as having lost the final sibilant of the nominative. Meister, I, 272; but cf. also p. 310.

ARCADO-CYPRIAN AND DORIC.

η, not ει (ē), is the result of compensatory lengthening. Arcadian ἦναι, φθήρων; Cyprian ἠμί. The dialects diverge in the treatment of ονς. But there is no example of ου (closed ō) for ω (*i.e.* open ō) of other dialects.

There is as yet no authority for an Arcado-Cyprian contraction of α + ε to η, as in Doric, Elean, and North Greek. See p. 81.

Spitzer's ascription to Arcado-Cyprian (p. 57) of the personal ending -ες in the indic. present, is based upon no foundation save that, as the Cyprian form is old, it might well have been a survival of an Arcado-Cyprian period. But a solitary instance is found: ἐς πόθ' ἔρπες· πόθεν ἤκεις. Πάφιοι. With this compare the Theocritean συρίσδες, I. 3, which is certain, and ἀμέλγες, IV. 3. This form occurs on no Doric inscription. Whether the form in -ς is proethnic (cf. Latin *legis;* old Irish, *do-beir,* *-beres*), or merely a Greek parallel to τίθης, has not yet been made out.

---

[1] The nom. ἱέρεως, Rev. Arch. XXVIII, 106, from λεώς; λεώ = ἱέρεω.

It is not improbable that the Arcado-Cyprian infinitive of -ω verbs ended in -ν; *e.g.* Arcad. ἰμφαίνεν (or ἰμφαῖνεν), Cypr. ἔχεν. As Deecke reads ἔχην in the single passage where any such formation occurs, the assumed parallelism between Arcadian and Cyprian must be left in dispute. Johansson, De verbis derivatis contractis, p. 202, accepts an Arcado-Cyprian ἔχεν, comparable to Doric κρίνεν, and to an Ionic ὀφείλεν (Cauer², 527). See p. 96.

ἰν for ἐν,[1] formerly held to be a distinctive peculiarity of Arcado-Cyprian, has now appeared upon a Cretan inscription. See Merriam, Am. Journ. Archaeol. III, 312. ἰγνύη was regarded by Curtius as standing for ἐγ-γνύα. ἐν, cum accus. and cum dat., is a relic of the period when this preposition was construed as the German *in*.[2] The Aeolic εἰς and Ionic ἐς (εἰς) gradually drove out this double construction. If the Aeolians of Lesbos ever used ἐς *cum genet.*, its obsolescence must have been caused by the adoption of the Ionic ἐκ, and have been subsequent to the period when ἐν *cum accus.* was replaced by εἰς *cum accus.*

ARCADO-CYPRIAN, DORIC, AEOLIC, AND CONNECTED DIALECTS.

1. Genitive plural, Â declension. *Arcad.* Ἀλεατᾶν, ἐργωνᾶν, Τεγεατᾶν. *Cypr.* ἐπαγομενᾶν. Here Homeric, Boeotian -αων, Thessalian -αουν, alone show the older form.

2. Genitive sing., O declension. *Arcad.* τῶ, *Cypr.* θεῶ. -οο must then have been open sounds at the period of contraction. On -ω, -ν, see pp. 68, 118. -οιο from epic reminiscence in Arcad., Roberts, No. 280.

3. The relative use of demonstratives. In *Arcadian* ὅπερ is used for ὅσπερ in 1222₃₆: ἔστω δὲ καὶ τωνὶ τῶ ἐπιζαμίω ὁ αὐτὸς ἴγγυος ὅπερ | καὶ τῶ ἔργω ἧς ἰν ἔστεισιν. With this compare the Homeric ὅ περ σέο πολλὸν ἀμείνων (VII, 114, XXI, 107), and the use of ὅτις, III, 279.

---

[1] ἰν > ἐν originally before consonants. ἐ for ἐ(ν) is found, Roberts, No. 277, according to the generally received reading. προσθαRε must be read πρόσθα[δ]ε. I cannot subscribe to Robert's defence of ἐ(μ) Μαντινέαι; cf. Allen, *Versification*, p. 150. Cyprian has no instance of ἐν, and the Arcadian cases are not unimpeachable. ἐν in 1200 is poetical; in 1231 it is the work of a meddler with the original text; 1183 is probably Arcadian, though peculiar in many ways; No. 1233, a proxeny decree, distinguishes ἐν from ἰν.

[2] Cf. ἰσς > ἰνς and ἰς *cum accus.* in Oaxos. Merriam l. l. In Gortyna ἐς *cum gen.* and *accus.*

In *Cyprian*, ὅ for ὅς in 60₁₂ : ἤ κέ σις 'Ονάσιλον ἐξ ὀρύξη, ἰδέ παι, ὅ ἐξ ὀρύξη, πείσει 'Ονασίλωι ; and also 60₂₅. Arcadian has no example of ὅ alone used for ὅς. ὅτινι, 1222₂₇, is the masculine form from ὅτις. τό is used as a relative, 1222₁₄,₈₅ ; τά in Cyprian, 68₄. This breaking down of the old demonstrative force is found outside of Homer and these dialects, in Ionic (Herodotus), in the Attic poets, perhaps in the language of the common people of Attica (cf. C. I. A. II, 611₁₁), in Doric, Elean, Aeolic, Thessalian, Boeotian, etc.

4. The participle of εἰμί. *Arcad.* ἐόντος, 1222₁₁. *Cypr.* ἐπιό(ν)-τα, 60₉,₁₉ ; ἰό(ν)τα, 60₂₃. ἐών is pan-Hellenic (Attic ὤν). Aeolic has both ἔων (Sappho 75 and on inscriptions) and ἔσσα (Sappho 75). Doric ἐών, Ahrens, II, 323.

5. Apocope of prepositions. *Arcad.:* πὰρ τάν, 1222₄₀ ; κάτ in κατάπερ, 1222₄₈,₅₀. *Cypr.* καλέχες · κατέκεισο Πάφιοι. Pamph. καθῆδυ, 1267₁₃. Aeolic καττά. Boeot. καττόν (κατά in late inscriptions). Thess. καττάπερ. Heraclean πὰρ Πανδοσίαν, I, 58. Cretan παρδέχεται, C. I. G. 3050₂₁. Delphic κατ τάν and κατάν, Cauer², 204₄₁ and ₁₁. Elean καδαλέοιτο.

6. ἧς third sing. imperfect : <ἦσ + τ. *Arcad.* 1222₃₇. *Cypr.* κεραμεὺς ἧς, Berl. Phil. Wochens., 1884, p. 671. Corcyraean, I. G. A. 342₃. Sicilian (Epicharmus 73, Ahrens), Doric (Alcman in the Mss. frag. 24), Aeolic (in Theocritus, XXX, 16) ; cf. Boeot. παρεῖς, 500₇. ἦν, whatever may be its origin, is certainly a later form.

7. η, by contraction of ε + ε in the augment, after the expulsion of σ, ϝ, or *yod*. Herein Doric, Arcado-Cyprian, and Aeolic, etc., are alike. Other vowel contractions are alike the possession of Arcado-Cyprian and of other dialects. *E.g. : —*

ᾰ + ω = ω, ᾰ + ο = ᾱ in all dialects except Ionic and in later North Greek. ᾱ + ο, ω = ᾱ, except in Attic-Ionic.¹ ᾰ + ε = η in Arcado-Cyprian probably,² in Doric, North Greek, and in Elean (?) ; = ᾱ in Aeolic, Boeotian, and Ionic. Johansson, De verbis derivatis contractis, p. 58, is doubtful about the Arcado-Cyprian contraction of α + ε. He, however, suggests η. -εος from -εσος (nom. -ης) remains open in both dialects, and in Cyprian does not become -ιος. See p. 109.

8. ε for α in ἱερο-. *Arcad.:* ἱερῶν, 1222₂₃ ; Ἱέρων, 1231, C 13, etc. ; with ἱαρής in 1235. *Cypr.:* ἱερῆϝος, 38₁ ; ἰϝερής, 33 ; ἱερέϝιγυαν, 60₂₀, etc. ἱερο- obtains also in North Greek, Doric (Cretan, Laconian), Thessalian, Boeotian, Ionic-Attic, Homeric. The Aeolic ἶρος

---

¹ In Boeotian when ᾱ + ω contract, ᾱ is the result, *e.g.* τᾱν, otherwise -αων.
² But cf. Cyprian ἰγᾶσθαι and ἐδίϝτα.

is either the descendant of ἱερος or of *ἱσρος < isṛrós. The older form
with a (cf. *ishirá*) is Arcadian,[1] Boeotian, Thessalian, Laconian, Heraclean, Messenian, Corcyraean, Cretan, and Theraean. Not only can
we not hold with Brand, De dialectis Aeolicis, p. 14, that the a form
is Doric solely, but we are even driven to admit that these words,
which have long been held to be a criterion of dialect differentiation,
are not entitled to this position from the early and wide-spread appearance of the form with ε. All necessity of assuming a "pan-
Aeolic" ἱερός and a "pan-Doric" ἱαρός, crossing in the various sub-
dialects, is obviated by the easy supposition that in the pre-dialectal
stage of Greek both forms existed side by side.

9. Vocalization of ϝ, as in *Arcad.* Φαυῖδας, 1246, C 17; Φαύλλω,
1246, A 15 ;[2] cf. φαύεα καλά in Homer, as Hartel correctly reads. Cf.
Cypr. ϝέσις, ναυ- in Ναυφάμω, Berl. Phil. Wochens., 1886, p. 1291, and
in ναύαρχος, if Deecke and not Voigt is right. Cypr. ναυ[άρχω], 160
(cf. 157), a title which is doubted by Voigt, B. B. IX, 171. νᾶον in
No. 41. Other examples of the vocalized labial spirant are Boeot.
Ἀρχεναυῖδας, Coll. 413₁₀ (a Pellenian); ὑρειγαλέον· διερρωγός; Σαυ-
γένεις, 914, IV, A;[3] Thessal. Ἑρμαύου, 1300; Laconian Λαναγήτα,
C. I. G. 1466; Aeolic, ναῦος, φανόφοροι (gramm.); Pamphyl. φάβος =
φάος, Heraclides; εὐιδε (Balbilla), etc. Deecke reads ϝευξάμενος, 45,
the ὐ of which Deecke and Ahrens compare with ἐπί. G. Meyer,
Gramm.², § 239, seems to regard ὐ as having some connection with
vocalized ϝ. Cf. Baunack's Studien, I, p. 16, 17, where ϝευξάμενος
is read, and the explanation from I.E. *ud* offered. Quantitatively considered, the examples of υ > ϝ are more frequent in the Aeolic than in
the dialects connected with Aeolic, and more frequent in the latter
than in Doric or Ionic.[4] Curtius holds that υ > ϝ is a proof of the
connection of Cyprian with Thessalian and Boeotian (Kleine Schrif-

---

[1] Since ιαρής occurs in 1235 alone, — an inscription in North Greek, — an
Arcadian ιαρής is uncertain. Bechtel remarks that this inscription is wholly
North Greek, with the exception of ιαρής. But this may point to a North Greek
-ης for -ευς; cf. above, p. 79. ιερ- occurs about thirteen times in Arcadian. ιαρ-
in Cyprian is doubtful, according to Meyer, Gramm.², § 94. But cf. yαρά, Hall
ιαρά, 72; Ἰαρώ(ν)δαυ, 118; ἰψαρώτατος, 41. The last example, at least, is not a
matter of dubitation.

[2] Cyprian here, Φοϝέω, 133.

[3] The σαυ- forms belong here only in case the explanation from αο be rejected;
cf. page 65. Fuhrer and Spitzer agree in abandoning the explanation of G. Meyer,
§ 120 (from αο). But Attic Λαυδικεύς speaks in favor of G. Meyer.

[4] Cf. Tudeer, De digammo testimonia, 68. •

ten, II, 156) ; that this is too narrow a view is shown by the Doric Λαναγήτα.

10. Aeolic, Elean, Laconian, etc., may, together with Arcado-Cyprian, have preserved an open $\bar{e}$ whose length, *e.g.* in contractions, appears as $\bar{e}$ (η). The short *e* sound may have become closed at a very early period, as in the North Greek dialects (generally) in Thessalian, Boeotian, and Ionic. Again in the preservation of the open $\bar{o}$ in its lengthened sound (ω = Ionic ov) these dialects agree. Boeotian here sides with Arcadian (but not in the accus. pl. <ovs) and with Cyprian (gen. -ω). Thessalian at an early date adopted the closed sound of the lengthened *o*.

11. *Arcad.* Τηλίμαχος, *Cypr.* Τηλεφάνω. Cf. Boeot. Πειλεστροτίδας (but also Τειλεφάνειος), Aeolic πήλυι, Delphic Πηλεκλέας. But there is no proof that the form with τ might not be Aeolic, as we have Aeolic πέντε as well as πέμπων. It is doubtless as much a matter of chance that we have no case of π followed by a dark vowel, which was the source of the later analogue πήλυι, as it is that τηλ- does not appear in Aeolic.

Arcado-Cyprian, Doric, Aeolic, Ionic.

Loss of intervocalic ι : *Arcad.* ποέντω, 1222₉ ; *Cypr.* 'Αθάνα (dat.), 62, through 'Αθαναία, which is Arcadian (1202), and 'Αθάναα (Alcaeus, 9) ; Cretan ὑγιέα ; Locr. ἀδελφεός ; Aeolic 'Υμήναον ; Thess. Γεννάοι ; Boeot. Πλαταεῖος ; Elean ἔα, συνέαν ; Ionic κέεται.

πέντε is the pan-Hellenic. Aeolic πέμπε does not exist despite the assertion of the grammarians. See below, p. 106.

Difference between Arcadian and Cyprian.

We have now exhausted the cases of agreement between Arcadian and Cyprian, and turn to a registration of their actual differences.

In order to present at a glance the dialect affinities of Arcadian and of Cyprian, in the following sections the differences between the two dialects will be so arranged as to give contributory evidence from all the other dialects with which either Arcadian or Cyprian may be in correspondence. Whenever an example of the phonetic law in question is found in either dialect, but as yet absent from the other, care has been taken to notice the fact.

I. Arcadian and Aeolic.

1. *o* for *a.*

δεκόταν, 1198; cf. Balbilla δεκότω (dat.), 323₅. The Aeolic inscriptions have δέκατος twice (as in Boeotian), once in an inscription dating from 16 B.C., once in one in the period between 2 B.C. and 14 A.D. Little can therefore be determined by epigraphic evidence whether or not that stadium of the dialect which was imitated by the court poetess of Hadrian had already assimilated the final syllables of δέκατος to -κοντα, producing δέκοτος. Cf. Ionic-Attic, Aeolic εἴκοσι from -κοστος. The analogy can scarcely have been felt to be operative in the time of Balbilla. It is certainly remarkable if the mere desire on her part to tinge her poems with an archaic flavor had resulted in the creation of form which actually appears in a dialect in many particulars akin to Aeolic.

There is no instance in the numerals of *o* for *a* in Cyprian. Despite δεκόταν, Arcadian holds with Boeotian *a* in -κασιοι (Boeot. -κατιοι).

NOTE. — On *o* for *a* in Arcad. Ἑκατόμβοια, see p. 105.

2. Refusal to weaken ε to ι before vowels.

The Aeolic cases, except perhaps the gen. γλύκιος, are all capable of another explanation. A ground form χρυσε-ιο-ς with accent on the ultimate (cf. ἀφ(ε)νειός) may produce χρύσιος through χρυσ(ε)ιός. The loss of intervocalic ι is amply attested for all Hellenic dialects. γλύκιος may perhaps represent a γλυκε(ϝ)ιός. On Cyprian ι<ε before vowels, see p. 109.

2. The terminations -αισι and -οισι have sometimes been regarded Aeolic. The infrequency of their appearance in Homer in comparison with the growth of -αις and -οις is indicative of an obsolescent formation; their prevalence in Aeolic literature and inscriptions, and their sparse appearance in Ionic (except Herodotus) and in Attic seemed to point a form that, quantitatively considered, might be called Aeolic. Arcadian Ἀλειοῖσι, 1183, is the only example of -οισι in this dialect. It has been supposed that No. 1183 was of Elean origin, but -οισι offers no support to this belief, as the Elean form is invariably -οις or -οιρ. See Kirchhoff, Alphabet,⁴ 159. I regard -οισι as pan-Hellenic, not Aeolic, and Ἀλειοῖσι as the sole survival in Arcadian of the locative case form, which in every Greek dialect gave place gradually to the instrumental -οις>-ōis. Ἀλειοῖσι cannot be a loan formation, since -οις was the accepted form in every neighboring dia-

lect at the time of this inscription (about 400). With the exception of the form for Ξ the alphabet is pre-Ionic. With the realization of the fact that -οισι and -οις are totally distinct case-forms, the attempt to extirpate -οισι from Homer falls to the ground. -αις and -οις are the forms in Cyprian, Thessalian, and in Boeotian (except No. 744, ξείνοισι, an epic reminiscence.). -οισι occurs in Doric only in poetry.

4. ἡμίσσοι, 1222 $_{25}$, with its σσ seems to recall Aeolic ἰσσο-θέοισι, 311 $_{15}$, of which the ground-form is found in Cretan ϝ]ισϝό-μοιρον (Gortyn. X, 50) = Skt. *viçu-*. It is preferable, however, to regard the form with σσ as pan-Hellenic, and sporadic in the Greek dialects. ἥμισσον occurs on a Chalcidian inscription, according to Ditten- berger, Hermes, XVI, 173. Where there is but a single σ, this may also arise from σϝ- ; and there is no need to assume a parallel stem, ἡμισο-. In North Greek we have ἥμισος in Phocis and in Delphi (Anecd. Delph. 38 (late)) ; ἥμισσον is, however, also Delphic ; cf. Wescher-Foucart, 126 $_{13}$, 213 $_{11}$. Aeolic αἰμισέων (*sic*, and not αἰμίσεων), 213 $_{9, 11}$. The Cyprian form of ἴσος is ἔϝεισος, 68.

5. Traces of Aeolic ψίλωσις cannot be discovered. Ἀλκίππω, not Ἀλχ-, since the spiritus asper of ἵππος is secondary. The same may be said of Πλειστίερος from the older ἱερός (*ishirá*), despite Ηιερόν, 1257 $_2$. Were any distinct traces present of the Arcadians having been ψιλωτικοί, as the Lesbians and Eleans, nothing would be proved as to their nearer connection, since even on the hypothesis of a North Aeolic dialect (Lesbian, Thess., Boeot.) the ψίλωσις of the Lesbians has to be referred to a period after the withdrawal of the Lesbic Aeolians.

II. ARCADIAN AND THESSALIAN.

In Arcadian we have -νι added to the demonstrative stem forma- tion ταν[ν]ί, 1222 $_{53}$. With this particle is connected the Thessalian -νε in τόνε τοὐννεουν τοίνεος. This νι is a result of the abstraction of ν + ι (ιδ) from such cases as τον-ί(δ), ταν-ί(δ), των-ί(δ) ; this -νι was then added to τάν (above). It is probable that Thessalian -νε is nothing more than this -νι(δ), though no sufficient reason can be adduced for the substitution of ε for ι.[1] The Thessalians appear to have had a fondness for the ε sound ; cf. διέ for διά, βέλλειται for βούλη- ται. Reference has already been made (p. 68) to the -ν of Cyprian genitive singular (ἀργύρων) and to its possible connection with this -νι or -νε.

[1] Baunack, Studien, p. 56, and note, page 68 above.

The form βέλλειτι renders apparent a tendency in each dialect to change ται, the personal ending of the middle, though the result is different. Arcad. -τοι (ἰνδικάζηται, 1222₃₄; γένηται, 1222₅; τέτακτοι; 1222₄₄). Thessal. -τει (βέλλειτει).

The treatment of vowel + nasal + ς in the different dialects is so varied that it is impossible to construct any system that shall take as its starting-point the ground-form (*e.g.* ανς, ονς) and nevertheless make clear the difference, in the treatment of this ground-form, between dialects that are otherwise patently allied to each other. In no one particular do the so-called Aeolic dialects diverge more widely : —

	ανς	ονς
Aeolic	παῖσα, ταίς	μοῖσα, τοίς
Thessalian . . .	πάνσα	ταγός
	ταμίας	
Boeotian . . .	δραχμάς	ἰώσας
Arcadian . . .	ἐργωνήσας	τὸς ἐπισυνισταμένος
	δαρχμάς	
Cyprian	τάς	τώς ?
Elean	μναῖς μνᾶς πᾶσα	τοίρ
	καταξίαιρ	

The quantity of -ας in Thessalian and Arcadian is supposed to be short[1]; in Boeotian, long. See Prellwitz, De dialecto Thessalica, p. 32, 33.

The Cyprian *to · se ·* is generally transcribed in Greek as τώς, doubtless on the analogy of *e · mi* as ἠμί, and from the assumed Doric character of compensatory lengthening in Cyprian. We have, however, no warrant for accepting τώς to the prejudice of either τό(ν)ς or, more probably, τός. If the parent Arcadian had τός, it is difficult to see how the influence of neighboring Doric speech could have been so powerful as to have displaced so common a form. Deecke formerly wrote τόνς (Curt. Stud. VII, 1875), as Cauer, in Wochens. für kl. Philol. 1884, p. 99; but in his Delectus[2], τός. But an Arcadian prototype is not as authoritative a criterion as might be desired, from the fact that both τός and κελεύωνσι exist side by side, though the latter, however, is a later form.

The dialects of Argos and of Crete are extremely instructive as

[1] Brugmann, Grundr. § 205, Anm. 2, assumes that the α was long. At the period when -ντι became -νσι there was no possibility of the ν disappearing, since the movement which created δαρχμάς had spent itself.

regards the chronology of -ανς, -ας, -ονς, -ος. In the older inscriptions of each dialect we find -ανς and -ονς;[1] in the later monuments, -ας and -ος. Hence any dialect which long preserved νς does not offer any trace of the influence of ν when it disappeared at a comparatively late date in the development of the dialect. But in those dialects in which ν vanished at an early date, compensatory lengthening serves to attest that early disappearance. Now were we certain of the Cyprian forms ἴω(ν)σι or ἴωσι, ἔξο(ν)σι or ἔξωσι (cf. p. 66), we might better compare Arcadian and Cyprian. If both preserved νσι (cf. Arcad. κελεύωνσι), the Arcadian and Cyprian forms would be τός and τάς, of which the former is actually preserved. Common usage, however, dictates Cyprian τώς, the parallel to which would be τάς.

The Doric dialect with its ᾱς and ᾰς, ως and ος show that both forms may coexist in prose and in verse.[2]

A comparison of indisputable forms suggests that Arcadian finds its nearest parallel in Thessalian among the dialects nearer akin to Aeolic, and in Doric (Argos, Crete, etc.). No one has as yet, I believe, committed himself to the statement that Arcadian τός is a loan form from a Doric dialect in which τόνς was long preserved, but finally passed into τός.

NOTE 1. — The difference between the dialects in their treatment of ν + secondary σ at the end and between vowels is briefly this: In Arcadia and Thessalia this νς is preserved intact. In a part of Crete and in Argos this νς is preserved intact, as also final ν + s. In all other dialects the nasal sound is expelled, leaving ι + s in Aeolic and in the rest s with preceding compensatory lengthening. But the relations of Arcadian and Cyprian are peculiar if the Cyprian form is in reality τάς, since, with κελεύωνσι and τός, we have all three forms. An Arcado-Cyprian τός and κελεύωνσι are reconcilable, but not an Arcado-Cyprian κελεύωνσι and τώς. If, however, ἴωσι and τώς are the Cyprian forms, Cyprian appears to have followed its own dictation, and there is no Arcado-Cyprian common form.

NOTE 2. — In δέατοι Arcadian has lost ϝ, as Thessalian in ποτεδέετο. Cf. Aeolic δεύω; Attic δείηται, C. I. A. II, 167₄₈, ₄₈ (334-325 B.C.).

[1] This orthography may be merely a traditional representation of the ground-form; and ᾱς, ος may have been spoken.

[2] ᾱς in Doric can be attested in poetry alone; ος occurs in Crete, Thera, Cyrene, Cos, etc.

ARCADIAN AND BOEOTIAN.

There are no specific points of contact between Arcadian and Boeotian. Their joint correspondences are of little value for the purpose of proving any direct relationship.

1. Dat. = loc. in -οι.

This is in reality pan-Hellenic, and has been assumed to be in use in Cyprian parallel to ωι, ω. See p. 73. Arcadian and Boeotian meet here solely in the fact that they have preserved a greater number of cases of -οι than any other dialect. -οι recurs in North Greek, later Elean, and Eretrian. In Doric and Attic-Ionic the -οι forms are held in check by the regular dative in -ωι. Cf. p. 100.

2. Arcadian shares with Boeotian, but chiefly with Doric, the imperative ending -ντω. See p. 95.

3. Arcadian: ἀν in ἀναλώμασιν, 1222₄₁; ἀγκαρυσ[σόντω], 1222₁₉; ἀνέθηκε, 1225; ἀνέθεν, 1229.

ἀν does not occur alone, nor is ἀνά found.

The Cyprian form is ὀν in ὀνέθηκε, 72, 74, 75, 120; ὀνέθηκεν, Tamassus, Berl. Phil. Wochensch., 1886, p. 1323 (ἰνέθηκε, 45, is doubtful). Either the κοινή form ἀνά or the Doric ἀν appears in ἀνέθηκε, 17, 76.

Cyprian herein ranks with Aeolic: ὀγκαρυσσέτω, 304₂₈₇ (Aeolic has in later inscriptions the κοινή form); and with Thessalian:[1] ὀν-γραφεῖ, 361₂₁₁. Boeotian has the Doric ἀν and the κοινή ἀνά. Elean has ἀνά as Ionic-Attic. This variation of Arcadian from Cyprian is one of the most salient differences between the two dialects, which, especially in the form and use of the prepositions, have preserved intact their kinship to the latest times. It is certainly surprising that ἀν in Arcadian should be due to Doric influence, whereas ἀπύ and ἐς, *cum dativo*, have been preserved.

4. ε for the common ο in Ἐρχομένιοι, 1212; cf. Boeot. Ἐρχομενός, the epichoric name of the Boeotian and of the Arcadian city. This too has been held to be an example of the general fondness for ερ among dialects of Aeolic coloring. The interrelation of ερ and ορ in this and similar words (*e.g.* Boeot. Τρεφία and Τροφία) has not yet been clearly made out.

5. Arcadian and Boeotian stand nearer in the gen. sing. Â decl. (Arcad. -αυ; Boeot. -αο, seldom ᾱ) than do Arcadian and Thessal.

---

[1] Thessaliotis and Histraeotis have ἀνά.

(ā) or Arcadian and Aeolic (ă). The traces of -ao in Cyprian are sporadic, cf. p. 65.

6. On Arcadian and Boeotian θεᾱρός, see p. 98. The Arcadian and Boeotian a in -κασιοι, -κατιοι, is a survival of the original form in a (see p. 99), and therefore no special mark of interrelation.

7. ἔμπασιν, 1234 (about 200 B.C.), an inscription almost entirely Hellenistic; ἵνπασιν, 1233; cf. Boeot. ἔππασιν about twenty-five times; ἔπασιν only 492₁₀, 719₈; Doric-Aeolic, ἔγκτησις. Cf. also ʼΑριστο-πάμων, 1231ₑ₇, 1248₄₃.

8. The Arcadian dialect displays the same variation in the form of the name of Dionysus as is observable in other dialects; Διονυσίω, 1203₁₂; Διωνύσιος, 1246, A 4. Neither Διόνυσος or Διώνυσος appears on any Cyprian monument. It is impossible to discover any dialect affinities in the varying forms of the Attic Διόνυσος. Ζόννυσος, Lesb.; Διόννυσος, Thessal; Διοννυσίαν, Cretan; Διοννυσόδωρος, Lesb.; Διωνύσιος, Thessal. Homer, Διώνυσος (except λ 325), which cannot be Doric, nor Ionic if compensatory lengthening from οσν took place, since Ionic never has ω for ου, nor ever had it, according to Johansson, p. 66. Pindar too has Διόνυσος once, Isth. VII, 5. Boeot., Διόνυσος; Elean, Διονυσιακοῖς; Heracl., Διόνυσος; Teos, Διόνυσος; Rhodes, Διοννυσιαστᾶν; Aetol., Διόνυσος; Διώνυσος in Homer, Hesiod, Theognis, Pindar, the tragedians, Theocritus.

It is therefore probable that, as in the case of Poseidon, the Greek language possessed originally double forms of this name, to explain which has baffled all efforts. Solmsen, K. Z., XXIX, 39, objects with justice to Baunack's explanation from δι-ονυχιος, but fails to offer any more convincing suggestion than that Διόνυσος had an σ interposed from Διός by popular etymology.

With Boeotian (and with Laconian), Arcadian possesses the οι diphthong in Ποσοιδᾶνος, Roberts, No. 276. Cf. Boeot. Ποτα[δ]ά-[ιχος]; Lac. Ποοῖδαια.

ARCADIAN, THESSALIAN, BOEOTIAN.

ϝϝις from ϝϝες in ϝιστίαν, 1203₁₈; Thessal. ʼΙστιαίε[ι]ος; Boeot. ʼΙσστιαίδας. This proves no necessary connection between these dialects, as the change of ε + σ + cons. + ι to ι + σ + cons. + ι occurs in Ionic, Locrian, Laconian, Cretan, and in Heraclean; and is not of very early date. It is so restricted geographically that it can scarcely be called pan-Hellenic. See Collitz in A. J. P., VII, 216.

The Attic ἑστία has not been imported into Aeolic (Coll. 215 47, 48) as has been assumed. In Attic ἐστ- is found upon the more ancient inscriptions. Cf. pp. 91, 109.

ARCADIAN, AEOLIC, THESSALIAN, BOEOTIAN.

Inflection of pure verbs according to the -μι class. ζαμιόντες, 1222 50; ζαμιώ[σ]θω, 1222 28, not ζαμιόσθω; from *ζαμίωμι, rather than from *ζαμιο + εσθω; ζαμιόντω, 1222 17 (cf. Johansson, p. 57); ποέντω, 1222 9; σ]τεφανώτω, Le Bas, 331 45 (not in Collitz); ἀδικήμενος, 1222 4; ἀδικέντα, 1222 4; [ἑλλαν]οδικόντων, 1257 11. The εω inflection has, however, not been entirely superseded; cf. διατελεῖ, 1252. Aeol. φιλήμενος; Boeot. ἀδικείμενος, at least at the time of Aristophanes; cf. Ach. 884. There is no certain example of the "Aeolic" inflection in Cyprian. Cyprian κατεϝόρκων, 60, is explained by Deecke as coming from καθορκέω; by Johansson from ϟαταϝορκόω. This inflection obtains also in North Greek: Delphic, ποιείμενος; Locrian, καλείμενος; Elean, κα(δ)δαλήμενος (Pamphylian, βωλήμενυς, may be from -α + εμενος). See A. J. P. VII, 441, where I have held that these forms cannot constitute a line of demarcation between different dialects. Johansson, De derivatis verbis contractis, p. 45, has shown that this so-called Aeolic inflection does not support any connection between North Greek and Thessal.-Lesb. He and Brugmann, Gramm., § 118, explain these parallel forms to ε-ο-μενος, as originating from ε-(ι)ε-μενος; cf. Osthoff, M. U. I, 212.

The fondness for the strong form ερ appears in ζέρεθρα, δέρεθρον, Ἐρίων, derivations from θέρσος, e.g. *Arcad.* Θερσίας, 1224, 1231, B 13; Θερσίλαος, Paus. VIII, 32, 1. *Aeolic* Θέρσιππος, 304. *Thessal.* Θέρσουν, Θέρσιος, Paus. V, 9, 1; Θέρσιππος. *Boeot.* Θερσάνδριχος, etc.[1] Neither θερσ- nor θαρσ- (θρασ-) occurs on any Cyprian inscription hitherto discovered; but in derivatives of κρέτος Cyprian ranks with Arcadian in possessing both the strong and the weak form.[2] It is an important point that only in the earlier inscriptions of dialects connected with Aeolic, in which the κοινή dialect has not forced an entrance, does this strong form come to light. From Doric inscriptions it is practically absent.[3] Quantitatively speaking, it is far more frequent

---

[1] Cf. Homeric Ἀλιθέρσης.

[2] Cf. also Cyprian ἔρ or ἔρ(α), ground form of ἄρα, ῥά, or ἄρ. τέρχνιϳα, 69 9, 19, 22 (cf. τρέχνος), appears also to have the strong form.

[3] θερσ- in a few Spartan proper names. θερσ- rarely in Attic-Ionic; a Corcyraean Θερσίλοχος, Paus. 6, 13, 6.

in dialects of Aeolic coloring. The influence of Doric or Attic is seen in Arcadian in Θρασέας, 1231, C$_{20, 89}$, 1250; Θράσιππος, 1249$_{10}$; Θρ]ασυμήδεος, 1231, A 33; Θράσων, 1189, A 35. See p. 70 for -κράτης. In Thessalian θαρσ- is less, in Boeot. more, frequent than θερσ-. It is, perhaps, more advisable to assume the influence of contiguous cantons, rather than suppose that the force of case levelling, which produced Homeric κάρτος and κράτος, had been kept alive with such tenacity as, in the second century B.C., to generate the weak forms. It should, however, not be suppressed that older and younger forms might have existed side by side until the latter proved all-powerful. The long life of older formations is seen in τριακάσιοι = Doric τριακατίοι, whereas α has given place to ο in Aeolic, Ionic, Attic, and, in fact, as early as the time of Homer.

NOTE. — ἐπιζαρέω, Arcadian, according to Eust. 909$_{27}$, is, however, also used by Euripides; cf. βαρύς. No strong form is in use.

The cases of retention of ερ should all be classed together, as Cyprian cannot be said to show any marked divergence here from the other dialects of the "Aeolic" type.

ARCADIAN AND IONIC.

ἄν may be either Doric or Ionic. It is certainly not Aeolic. It occurs in conjunction with κέ in Homer, and in Arcadian alone.[1]

εἰ sixteen times in 1222, and in no other inscription. There is no trace of αἰ, which occurs in older Doric, Elean, Aeolic, Boet. (ἠ), Homer (αἴ κε, αἰ γάρ, αἴθε). Is αἰ in Homer also Ionic? εἰ is Ionic and Attic, and often met with in later Doric inscriptions; once in Heraclean, I, 127. αἰ : εἰ : : svaí, Osc. : sī < svei, according to G. Meyer, § 113. For a discussion on αἰ, εἰ, and Cypr. ἠ, see above, p. 72.

Allusion has been made on pp. 89, 109 to the stem ἰστ (ϝιστ) for ἐστ-, found in Arcadian, Homer, Herod., Thessalian, Boeotian, and Doric.

NOTE. — A curious mixture of Arcadian and Ionic is found in Cauer², No. 537; cf. Roehl, 532, 533; Fick., Odyssee, p. 10: Μεσσή]νιος ϝοικέων ἐν Τεγέῃ| [θεοῖς πᾶσι]ν καὶ θεαῖς πάσαις. . . .

[1] For an assumed possible case in Cyprian, see p. 72.

ARCADIAN AND DORIC.

Many of the instances of parallelism between Doric and Arcadian will, upon close examination, be found to consist of phenomena which are pan-Hellenic, or existing merely to a greater extent in Doric than in other dialects. As a large number of the phenomena of Arcadian has been claimed as Doric, I have thought it proper to discuss their assumed Doric character in the following sections.

1. Compensatory lengthening. φθήρων, 1222₁₇; ἐγκεχηρήκοι, 1222₁₂, from ἐγχήρημι, the Arcadian counterpart of Attic ἐγχειρέω; cf. ἐκεχηρία in Delphic, Cauer², 204₄₈,₄₉. φθέραι, 1222₈, and φθήρων stand in such irreconcilable contrast that it is probable the ε of the former is due to an orthographical slip, though as a rule No. 1222 is remarkably free from blunders. Another case where an error on the part of the engraver has been assumed is διακωλύσει. See p. 101 for a discussion of this form. φθέραι < *φθέρσαι is supposed by Brand, p. 75, to have descended from a "pan-Aeolic" period, in which *φθέρσαι existed, and in the same way as κόρα from κόρϝα; cf. below, note 3. If ρ + σ was long retained, Brand maintains the expulsion of σ would be followed by no lengthening of the preceding vowel. ρσ (and λσ?) certainly did hold ground longer than did νσ, μς. Thus, for example, ἔκειρε must be explained as an analogue to ἔκτεινε, and ἔκερσε as a survival of the pan-Hellenic period. As ρσ became ρρ at an early date in Aeolic (though it was preserved in Ionic and old Attic), and as there is not a single example of the simplification of this ρρ, no twisting will make φθέραι out of φθέρραι. Nor is there any instance of the direct expulsion of σ from ρσ. As ρσ is retained in the aorist in poetry alone, except in case of the Cyprian ἔκερσε, 31, 32, Thessalian κόρα offers no support to Brand's hypothesis.

Ἀμηνέας, 1242, and Ἀμ]εινίαν, 1231, A 38, are irreconcilable forms in one and the same dialect. Either one or the other form is a loan form or contains an error of the stone-cutter. If we collect the evidence from the other Greek dialects as to the character of the sound preceding the ν of ἀμείνων, it appears that there is testimony in favor of ει as a genuine and as a spurious diphthong. EI is written C. I. A., I, 324 c; 138₁; 446₃₄; 447₄₇; 40₁₂. In Roehl, 372₁₀ (Styra), 390 (Amorgos), EI also occurs. But Cyprian Ἀμηνίϳα, 60₁₈, speaks in favor of an Arcado-Cyprian *ἀμήνων*. On Boeotian inscriptions we find Ἀμεινοκλεῖος, 571; Ἀμεινίαο, 571, and 807 ₂₄, appendix; Ἀμει[νο]-κλεῖος, 549 ₃, — all of the period of Ionic alphabet. But one form with EI antedates the introduction of the new alphabet: Ἀ]μεινο-κλείαε, 902. Of the twenty-five forms with Ἀμιν-, but one (Ἀμινο-κλέεις, 914, III, 8) is written in the older alphabet, and but one in the transitional period (Ἀμινάδαο, 700 ₁₀). All the others are in the Ionic alphabet. Meister (Dial. I, 222) holds incorrectly that the forms in ει are from η, which arose by compensatory lengthening, thus failing to account for the EI of the old Attic alphabet.

In no period of the Greek language which is free from itacism (and Arcadian has but two examples — πλήθι ἱράναι[1] — of the itacistic stage) is there any interrelation between genuine η and genuine ει.[2] It is only in the age of Augustus that we find an η for ει, an η wnich is distinctly due to Latin influence.[3] Nor does Cyprian, despite its ϝήπω, change genuine ει to η, as Deecke maintains. See p. 115. It is nevertheless true that there are cases in which η and ει appear side by side, as in Arcadian, Πλειστίερος, 1181, A 30; Πλη-στίερος, 1249 ₁₁; Πλείστ[ου], 1252 ₃ and Π]λήσταρχος, 1249 ₅.[4] Here the ει is undoubtedly as genuine as that of ἀμείνων. Cf. Roehl, 119 ₁₀, 532, 62 a Add.; C. I. A. I, 40 ₅₁, 55, 64 b ₁₂. It is conceivable that by shifting, the η of *πλη-ιων forced its entrance into the superlative πλεῖστος < *πλη-ιστός, but in the case of Ἀμηνέας Ἀμηνίγα, there is no point of departure for an η to supplant the original ει. The difficulties in the way of explaining these irregular forms are enhanced by the fact that the etymology of ἀμείνων is still uncertain.[5] Latin *mānus*, Sanscrit *samāna*, Lithuanic *aimieus* or *mainas*, have been tried and found wanting. The comparison of *melius* is certainly to be rejected. *amoenus* seems to explain the mutation vowel as EI, but its source is as obscure as that of the Greek word.

Doric procedure is also adopted in the unique ἦναι < ἐσ + ναι, 1222 ₁₀, 1233 ₂ [1257 ₃], with the spurious η of ἦμεν, which is Cretan, Heraclean, Elean, Boeot. (εἶμεν = ἦμεν), and also late Laconian.

---

[1] ἠρήνα or ἠράνα demanded by Spitzer, p. 34, are impossibilities.

[2] Thus τέθεικα is not from τέθηκα, but from analogy to εἶκα. η in Ἐλήθυια for Ἐλείθυια does not occur till the itacistic period. G. G. A., 1887, p. 442.

[3] Meisterhans, p. 22.

[4] ΚΛΕΤέας, Roberts, No. 282 = Coll. 1200, is uncertain. For other forms in πλει — and πλη — cf. below, p. 115.

[5] Meinck, De epenthesi graeca, 18–20, is unsatisfactory.

-ναι belongs to Homeric, Attic, and Ionic, but in no instance to Doric. See p. 69.

NOTE 1. — If ἤ-ναι is not from *ἐσναι, as seems probable, it may be a new formation from ἤ-μεν. This view is suggested by G. Meyer, and accepted with hesitation by Solmsen, K. Z., XXIX, 71.

NOTE 2. — Arcadian ξενο- is met with in the beginning of seventeen proper names and in two at the end. If Arcadian follows the laws of Doric compensatory lengthening, we should expect ξηνο-, or later ξεινο-, from a base ξενϜο-, which occurs frequently in other dialects. In fact, as Doric has both ξηνο- and ξενο-, North Greek ξεινο- and ξενο-, Boeotian ξεινο-, we are either compelled to assume a double formation ξενϜο- and ξενο-, or to hold that when Ϝ remained till a late period, it could disappear without leaving any trace of its former existence; but if the Ϝ of νϜ disappeared in certain dialects at a very early period, in certain words it produced either νν or compensatory lengthening of the preceding vowel. In poetry, however, the reduction of a geminated liquid or nasal may always ensue. Polybius, IV, 3, gives as a leader of the Aetolians Δορίμαχος (cf. C. I. G. 941, Attic). But we find Δωρίμαχος in an Acarnanian inscription, Coll. 1389. Ahrens' views (II, 171) on this point must be modified. The Attic form may have arisen from ξένϜος, it is true, but a Doric archetypal form ξένϜος can never have resulted in ξενο-. Cyprian has no certain instance of any form of the word ξένος. In Hall, Rev. No. 10 (A. O. S., XI, 235), a very doubtful inscription is read either Ϝεκὼν ἃ Ἔρωτι or τὰ ξένα Ἔρωτι (ἔρρο(ν)τι), the character χε· having no middle stroke.

NOTE 3. — A similar violation of Doric laws of compensatory lengthening appears to exist in Μελιχίωι, Cauer,[2] 464; Brugmann (Gramm. § 137), and Cauer, *ad loc.*, hold that φθέραι and Μελιχίωι are to be explained alike. Though it can be shown that the regular procedure of Doric in adopting a purely quantitative change of the α ε ο sounds in compensatory lengthening and in contraction with themselves, is more frequently violated than is generally supposed, in this case the analogy of Μελιχίωι for Arcad. φθέραι is worthless. Wilamowitz has referred the inscription to Arcadia (Zeits. f. Gymnasialwesen, XXXI, 648), but this has not been adopted by Bechtel, doubtless on the ground that the dative in -ωι is contrary to the genius of the dialect.

As regards the possible unity between all the "Aeolic" dialects, it cannot be shown on the score of Arcadian possessing ε̄ (*i.e.* ε̄ open) that the Arcadians left the assumed common home before Lesbians, Thessalians, and Boeotians changed ε̄ to ε̄ (ε̄ closed), since it cannot even be demonstrated that the three latter peoples did effect such a change either at one period or in the same place. Whether σπέρρω had become σπῆρω (open ε̄) in the Doric dialects by the time that the Arcadians are held to have reached Arcadia in their supposed prehistoric immigration from the north, whether the Arcadians adopted this σπῆρω instead of their traditional σπέρρω, or whether they themselves abandoned their σπέρρω of their own accord, can never be settled. It is probable, as far as the so-called Aeolic dialects are concerned, that they all possessed the form σπέρρω before their separation (assuming for the moment the breaking up of an original unity); whereas the Doric dialect before its division must have already accepted σπῆρω.

2. Third plural imperative in -ντω.

The examples in question occur in 1222 alone: διαγνόντω, l. 8;[1] ποέντω, 9; ζαμιόντω, 17; ἀγκαρυσ[σόντω], 19; ἰναγόντω, 19.

This termination of the imperative recurs in inscriptions of Laconia, Delphi, Messenia (Andania), and Rhodes. Cf. Boeot. οὐπερδι-κιόνθω, etc. The Lesbian termination is -ντον (στείχοντον, κατάγρεν-τον).

3. δαμιοργοί, 1181₉, recalls the same form in Messenian (Cauer,[2] 47₁₁₉), Achaean (Cauer,[2] 274; C. I. G. 1542₁₃, 1543₂₁, 1567₃₂), Locrian (Coll. 1479, 1480), Megarian (Bull, de Corr. Hellen. IX, 269, and Cauer,[2] 104₁₉), which was written under the dominion of the Achaean league;[3] and in inscriptions from Cnidus (Cauer,[2] 166, 167₈,₉), Telos (Cauer,[2] 169), Rhodes (doubtful, as δαμιΟΥΤήσας is found, Cauer,[2] 187, and δαμιουργήσας, Foucart, Rev. Arch. XIV, 333, n. 59, Camirus).[4] δαμιοργίσωσα is met with in Pamphylian (Collitz, 1260 and 1261; cf. also Ὀλόντιοι in Cretan, C. I. G. 2554₃). While more abundant on Doric territory, the existence of the vowel shortening before two consonants in Ionic must free this Arcadism from the suspicion of being herein tinged with a Doric peculiarity. As a matter of fact, δαμιωργός occurs in Doric,[5] Locrian (according to Roehl, 322₁₅ = Coll. 1479, where Bechtel has ο), and in Elean (Roehl, 122₂ = Coll. 1170). Cauer has attempted, in the Wochens. für klass. Phil., 1885, n. 26, to read ζαμιοργία for ζαμιωργία in Elean. The reading of Blass (No. 1152) is, however, not to be rejected; cf. also Ὀπ]οντίων (Roehl, 321), for Ὀπωντίων, Curt. Studien, III, 238.

NOTE. — The explanation of long vowel + sonant + consonant becoming short vowel + sonant + consonant is amply satisfactory (see Johansson, De derivatis verbis contractis, p. 20; Osthoff, M. U. I, 238; Perfect, 84, 196, etc.), and distinctly preferable to the assumption of a karmadhāraya compound, *δαμι(ο)ϝοργός.

4. Arcadian and Boeotian ἀν = ἀνά, as in Doric. Brand, De dialectis Aeolicis, p. 43, attributes the presence of ἀν in both these idioms to Doric influence. This cannot, however, be made out with any certainty. See p. 88.

---

[1] This form occurs I. G. A. 68, on the Laconian inscription from Tegea.
[2] Ahrens, I, 234, called the ο for ω/ου here a peculiarity of Achaean.
[3] An Achaean magistrate is referred to.
[4] Cauer restores δαμιοργός in a much mutilated inscription from Argos (Delectus, No. 48).
[5] δαμιουργός in the so-called Doris Mitior, C. I. G. 1193.

5. Infinitive in -εν. ἰμφαίνεν (or ἰμφαῖνεν), 1222₂₄; ἐπηρειάζεν, 1222₄₆; ὑπάρχεν, 1222₅₃. This form is not attested outside of Tegea. The Cyprian *e·ke·ne·* is the subject of much dispute. Deecke reads ἔχην, Johansson ἔχεν, doubtless to establish an Arcado-Cyprian ground-form in -εν, which is very tempting. Until the question is definitely settled, I have not compared an Arcado-Cyprian ἔχεν with a Doric ἔχεν. This termination has come to light in Cretan, Heraclean, Theraean, and in Delphic, though Cauer,[2] 204, contains the only example in the last-named dialect. ἀναγράφεν in Locrian, Coll. 1508, is perhaps a slip. It will, however, be necessary to reconstruct our ideas as to the diffusion of this infinitive ending, which will have to be regarded as pan-Hellenic, if we can obtain an absolutely certain example of its appearance in Ionic. At present, however, ὀφείλεν (Cauer,[2] 527 = Bechtel, Ionische Inschriften, No. 71) is the only example we possess. Bergmann, who first published the inscription, wrote ὀφείλεν; Cauer, ὀφείλι(ι)ν; Spitzer (p. 54), ὠφείλεν. Bechtel places the inscription in the fourth century, on account of the use of E for the spurious diphthong, thus reading ὀφείλειν. For a discussion of the origin of the infinitive -ν and -εν, see Johansson, p. 202.

6. It has been assumed that both Arcadian and Cyprian have ξ in the aorist of -ζω verbs. In proof thereof, Arcad. παρετάξωνσι, 1222₂₈ (from παρετάζω, according to Gelbke, p. 38, and not from παρατάσσω, as Bergk maintains) is adduced, together with Cyprian ἐξ ὀρύξη, 60₁₂. The latter form is referred by Curtius, Verbum,[2] II, 298, to ἐξορίζω and ὅρϝος, and explained as the equivalent of Attic ἐξορίσῃ. This explanation was adopted by Deecke and Sigismund (Stud. VII, 252); but Deecke has now retracted his former statement, and derived ἐξ ὀρύξη, as he writes the word, from ὀρύττω. ὡρίσετυ, 126, κατεσκεύϝασε, 31, speak against a Doric ξ in Cyprian.

The peculiarity of the Doric dialects in their treatment of -ζω verbs is this: when -ζω arises from a non-guttural stem, Doric follows the analogy of the guttural stems, and has ξ in the future and aorist. But Ionic-Attic has σ even when the verbal stem ended in a guttural, thus following the analogy of the dental stems. διαρπάξαις in Aeolic (Coll. 281) is therefore a survival of the original formation, which even in Homer had yielded to the σ form (ἥρπασε by the side of ἥρπαξε); cf. Cauer, in Sprachw. Abhand. hervorgeg. aus Curtius' Gramm. Gesellschaft, p. 147.

NOTE. — The method of affecting compensatory lengthening, ἀν for ἀνά, and the presence of ξ in the aorist of a verb with ζ in the present stem, are the only cases in Arcadian of contact between that dialect and those phenomena which have been held to be the characteristic marks of all the dialects of the Doric type, and to separate them from all others. There is no case of -τι, of the future in -ιω or -εω, as in πραξίω πραξεῖς, or of -μες for -μεν.

In many cases where Doric influence has been assumed, the phenomenon in question is in reality originally pan-Hellenic, but in the course of time has come to be the possession of a limited number of dialects. Thus, for example, we find the dual in Arcadian, φίλε, 1242, ἑλλαν]οδικόντοιν, 1257₁₁.[1] See Fick, G. G. A., 1883, p. 120; Roberts, No. 285. The fact of the early disappearance of the dual from Aeolic is not to be urged against a possible relationship between Aeolic and Arcadian, in favor of a closer connection between Doric and Arcadian.

Ἀπελλίων, 1190, based upon Ἀπέλλων, suggests Doric influence. Ἀπέλλων is ascribed to the Dorians by Herodian (II, 418, 25), and is found extensively upon Doric monuments (Crete, Laconia, Pamphylia, Megara, Syracuse); Ἀπελλαῖος occurs in Crete, Heraclea, Delphi; Pamph. Ἀπέλωνα. Were it not, however, for the existence of parallel names in Tenos, Colophon, Chios, Teos, Naucratis (Gardner's Naucratis, I, plate XXXII, 104), this Arcadian Ἀπελλίων might be held to be a loan form, especially as the Ionic, Attic, Aeolic, Boeotian, Cyprian (with the exception mentioned below) Ἀπόλλων prevails in Arcadia. The existence at the same time in one and the same dialect of the mutation forms Ἀπέλλων and Ἀπόλλων shows that in the period antedating the division into dialects, both forms must have existed, and that either one or the other was preferred in different parts of Greece,[2] though not to the entire exclusion of the other. A third form, Ἄπλων, is found in Thessalian (Ἀπλουνι) alone (cf. p. 108); a fourth form, Ἀπείλων, from Cyprus (Deecke in Berl. Phil. Wochenschrift, 1886, p. 217), is also *sui generis*.

This remarkable form with ει, I have attempted to explain below, p. 115. On the name Ἀπόλλων, see Prellwitz in B. B., IX, 327 ff. I can see no reason whatsoever for adopting Schröder's etymology, whereby Vedic Saparyeṇya and Ἀπέλλων are connected.

Spitzer holds that Arcadian follows Doric laws of contraction, but in most cases the result of the concurrence of vowels is not different in Doric from that in Aeolic, *e.g.* ā̆ + ω = ā̄ in ἐργωνᾶν; cf. τᾶν μοί-

---

[1] Cf. δύο ἔργα, 1222₂₆. At best the dual has no strong hold in Doric; cf. Lac. ἐπακόω, I. G. A. 83; ἐπάκοε, 86, like φίλε above (δύε for δύο, I. G. A. 69₇).

[2] The Doric dialects held fast to the form which best represents the strong forms of the old inflection: nom. Ἀπέλλων, gen. Ἀπλένος, voc. Ἄπολλον.

σαν in Aeolic. Ἐρμ[ᾶνο]ς, Roberts, 276; cf. 251, Laconia, and on
a bronze boar's head from Arcadia, now in Winterthur. νικῶν, Roberts, No. 280, is epic. In Boeotian, substantives still preserve the
open form (δραχμάων), Thess. κοινάουν.[1] So ε + ε, η + ε, etc., are
alike in Doric and in Aeolic. Medial ᾱ + ο = ᾱ[2] as in κοινᾶνας,
1222₂₁; Aeolic ᾱ + ο = αο or ω or ᾱ (Κρονίδᾱ, ᾶς, Λαχάρης); =
Doric ᾱ. cf. p. 81.

Gelbke, p. 17, asserts that Arcadians and Boeotians agree with the
Dorians in having ᾱ where other dialects have ω. Of the examples
quoted, Θεαρίδας, 1211 ₂,₄, calls for attention. θεαρός prevails in Laconian, Cretan, Delphic, Aetolian, Elean (θεαροίρ), Boeotian, etc.;
θεωρός in Ionic, Attic, and Aeolic. θεᾱρός is from θεα + ορος; θεωρός is from analogy to θυρωρός (Sappho, 98) > θυρᾱ + ορος, cf. θυρα-
ϝορός, Deecke, B. B., IX, 251. Doric, Boeotian, and Aeolic, contract
ᾱο to ᾱ, though Aeolic may leave ᾱο uncontracted. So far, then, from
sharing here any marked allegiance to Boeotian, the Arcadian Θεαρίδας fails to prove this assertion.

The ablaut form Ποσοιδᾶνος, 1217, finds its parallel in Boeot. Πο-
τοι[δ]ά[ϊχος], 474₁₂, and in Laconian Ποοῖδαια. The Aeolic form has
the middle ablaut form ει (Ποσείδαν). The οι form is equally original.
Collitz suggests (Verwantschaftsverhältnisse der gr. Dialekte, p. 14)
that the Laconian name Ποοιδάν must have been borrowed from the
Arcadians or from a people of similar dialect, since the genuine Spartan appellation of the sea-god in Sparta was Ποτιδάν or Ποτειδάν.
Brand asserts the direct contrary: — that the Arcadians borrowed the
Laconian form. But as the σ for τ is found on Doric territory (Ποσειδάν, Herodian, II, 916; Bull. de Corr. Hell. 1884, p. 355 ₂₄; Argolic Ποσιδάων, Cauer,[2] 58), it is possible that it is not necessary to
have recourse to an Arcadian Ποσοιδάν. The interchange of τ and σ
is due to a levelling of the original relations: τ + ι became σ in the
genitive and dative; whence σ before ει and οι, where τ originally
belonged. Or the τ maintains its ground before ει and οι, and in turn
supplants σ<τ + ι. From this we have Doric Ποτειδάν, Ποτιδᾶς,
Ποσειδάν, Ποσιδάων, Prellwitz, B. B., IX, 331).

Circumscribed within the confines of no narrow dialect boundaries,
though frequently allowed in Doric (Curt. Verb.[2] I, 75), are the past
tenses in -ν of the non-thematic conjugation: as, ἀνέθεν = ἀνέθεσαν,

---

[1] Ἀλκμᾶν, 1181, B 24, is also Doric; cf. Ποτιδάν < ᾱ + ο. The Aeolic form
represents the ante-contraction period.

[2] ᾱ + ο as final sound = αυ in Arcadian and Cyprian; = ᾱ in a medial syllable.

1229, 1230, 1258. This formation appears in Homer, Hesiod, Simon. Ceos, Pindar, but is rare in the tragedians; in inscriptions we find it in Messenian, Argolic, Heraclean, Laconian, and Delphic. Bœot. ἀνέθεαν has a different personal ending (αν(τ)) from ἀνέθεν (-ν(τ)).

δέᾱτοι, 1222₁₀ (οἱ δὲ στραταγοὶ πόσοδομ ποέντω, εἰ κ᾽ ἂν δέατοί σφεις πόλεμος . . .); 1222₁₈, ὅσαι ἂν δέατοί σφεις ζαμίαι; 1222₄₆, εἰ δ᾽ ἂν τις . . . ἐπηρειάζεν δέατοι ἰν τὰ ἔργα.

ἐπισυνίστᾱτοι, 1222₁₅,₁₆, is another example of the same formation, which is pan-Hellenic (not from *δεα + η + τοι, etc.[1]) and the original form of the subjunctives. Similar forms, illustrative of this primitive type of subjunctive before analogical influences had broken down their ancient structure, may be found in Curt. Verb.[2] II, 81; Johansson, De verbis derivatis, p. 69. Their geographical horizon embraces besides, Pindar, Pyth. IV, 92; Hipponax, 194; Hesiod, Aspis, 377; Dreros, Cnossus, Gortyna, Thera, Calymnia, Andania (five examples). It is thus a matter of chance that Doric seems to have been most tenacious of this ancient morphological heirloom. Certainly no connection of the Tegeans with Crete (Paus. VIII, 53, 4) can establish a connection of the Cretan with the Arcadian form. Nor is the Messenian form evidence of its existence in Sparta, whence Crete was colonized.

The peculiar form of the vocatives of -ες stems calls for comment, as it is in direct contrast to the Aeolic scheme of inflection. Ἀτέλη, 1205; Πολυκλῆ, 1206: cf. Ἀγαθοκλῆ, 1243; cf. C. I. G. 1148, Argol. In the Theogony of Hesiod, we find Κυπρογένη. To what dialect, if to any specific one, this form of the vocative is to be referred, is uncertain. The Aeolic tendency to metaplastic inflection avoids recourse to the Ā declension, preferring the O declension. Cf. Σώκρατε, Ἀριστόφανε, Joh., Gramm., 245; Greg. Corinth, 617; Gram. Meerm, 662. The analogy of αἰναρέτης, voc. αἰναρέτη, produced the vocative in -η instead of -ες. Other examples of this vocative are Σωσικλῆ, C. I. G. 3114, Teos; Ἀριστοκλῆ, C. I. G. 1154, Argolis; Διοκλῆ, Kaibel, 299, Erythrae; Δαμοκράτη, K 949, Sparta; Διομήδη, K 1124, Pompeii; Σωκράτη, C. I. G. 1150, Argolis; Ἑρμοκράτη, Mittheil. d. arch. Inst. VI, 129; Μενεκράτη, C. I. G. 1153, Argol; Ἑρμογένη, C. I. G. 9689, Rome, etc.

τριακάσιοι, 1222₈, has preserved the original α of the -κάτιοι of the Heraclean, Delphic, Boeotian, Laconian (-κάτιοι), Elean ([(π)]εντακα-τίων), Pamphylian (φίκατι), etc., while it has permitted assibilation.

---

[1] δέᾱτοι is subjunctive to δέατο, ζ 242. Cf. δεάμην· ἐδοκίμαζον.

The change of τι to σι is, however, chiefly prevalent in those dialects (Aeolic, Ionic, Attic) which have substituted ο for α through analogy to -κοντα. This form, then, is, as it were, the meeting-point of two series of dialects, Aeolic and Ionic-Attic. Arcadian τριακάσιοι offers no proof of an original Aeolic dialect, which changed α to ο through Ionic influence.

A few points calling for brief comment may now be added : —

λελαβηκώς, 1222₁₄ = Attic εἰλαφώς, has been held to be a Dorism, since μεταλελάβηκα occurs in Archimedes. See Ahrens, II, 347. λελάβηκα is used, however, by Herodotus and by Eupolis.

ἀφεώσθω, 1222₁₄. ἀφέωκα [1] is said by Suidas to be Doric (and Ionic). Herodian, II, 236₂, calls ἀφέωκα Doric. Cf. ἀνἐῶσθαι, Tab. Heracl. I, 152, and Hdt. II, 165, ἀνέωνται, in Cod. F with ω of the strong form, as in ἀνἐῶσθαι, ἀφέωμαι (Herodian, II, 236). ἀφέωκα, ἀφέωμαι are called Attic by Et. Mag. 176, 51, and by Et. Gud. 96, 11. See Ahrens, II, 344.

It will scarcely be maintained that because ος<ονς occurs in Arcadian and in Thessalian alone, of all the dialects that are in touch with Aeolic, that therefore Arcadian is tinged with Dorism. It is, on the other hand, probable that these dialects possessed ονς in their earliest stage, and transformed it according to individual preference, some changing before others the open ο before νς to a closed sound. See above, p. 86.

Pan-Hellenic are the so-called datives in -οι, in reality locatives, which have usurped the function of the allied case. *Arcadian:* ἔργοι, 1222₃,₄₉,₅₄; χρόνοι, 1222₄₂; αὐτοῖ, 1222₂, 1233₂,₆; τοῖ in 1222 six times, 1256; πολέμο[ι, 1233₅. In Arcadian there is no case of ωι. The same displacement of the dative occurs in Boeotian, (δάμοι, δάμοε, δάμυ,) in Phocian, Epirotic, Acarnanian, Aetolian (see A. J. P. VII, 431), and in Elean, δάμοι, 1153₇, 1156₄, 1159₈. Aeolic has ω, from ωι, in inscriptions; Thessalian, ου, from ω(ι). Cf. p. 73.

It is unsafe to conclude with Schrader, in Curt. Stud. X, p. 274, that the αι of φθέραι (cf. p. 92), 1222₈, is a proof of the Doric character of the dialect. φθέραι is preceded by διακωλύσει: εἰ δὲ πόλεμος διακωλύσει τι τῶν ἔργων ... ἢ τῶν ἠργασμένων τι φθέραι. διακωλύσει has been taken as a future by Bergk (Commentatio, p. xv) and by Schrader; but I know of no law of Greek syntax with which such a construction is in accordance. If a future, it is due to a bad slip on

[1] From ἔ-ω-α, with ablaut of ή.

the part of the stone-cutter.[1] Gelbke thinks with Michaelis that ε has been omitted through the inadvertence of the stone-cutter. Reading διακωλύσειε, he compares τύψειε. We have already assumed that φθέραι contains an error (p. 92), and this observation is, perhaps, to be extended to the remarkable form διακωλύσει. As an optative, this form cannot be shown to exist in Aeolic or Doric. See Curt. Verb.[2] II, 293 ; G. Meyer, Gramm.[2] § 593. Brugmann has offered the only explanation of the form as it stands (Morph. Untersuch. III, p. 66). κωλύοιαν (cf. El. ἀποτίνοιαν) : γράψειαν : : κωλύοι : *γραψει (*i.e.* διακωλύσει). But there are patent defects to this, as also to Spitzer's assumption of a samprasrana of ιε to ι or of ειε to ει in Arcadian.

Arcadian πρόσθα (Coll. 1200 ; Roberts, 277) seems to be Doric, as Aeolic literature and inscriptions have only -θε and -θεν. cf. Thessal. ἔμπροσθεν. But as -θα is cited as Aeolic by Joh. Alexandrinus (τονικὰ παραγγέλματα, 33 10), there is no doubt but that the -θα form is both Aeolic and Doric. Cf. Hom. ὔπαιθα, Fick, G. G. A., 1883, p. 120. Brand's conjecture, πρόσθε, is wide of the mark. There is no proof that " θα was changed to θε in a pan-Aeolic dialect."

Arcad. μέστε or μέστα, 1222 30 (μέστ' ἂν ἀφῆ[τοι] τὰ ἔργα). Cf. Cretan μέσ˘α κὰ ά κρίσις ἐπιτελεσθῇ, Cauer,[2] 120 39 ; μέττ' ἐς, Gortyn, IX, 48. Homer has μέσφα. Thessalian μέσποδί κε, 345 13 = ἔως ἄν. Baunack (Studien, p. 23) attempts to explain μέττες (*sic*) as resulting from μέχρι + ἐττε<ἐστε, in the sense of μέχρι εἰς ὅ. He has, however, forgotten that in Thessalian the interrogative form of the pronoun is used, not for the simple, but for the compound, relative. Prellwitz, G. G. A., 1887, p. 438–441, explains μεσ- as μετ + ς ; cf. πός<ποτ + ς (μες- : μετά : : ποτ : ποτί and πετά).

The change of φ and π in Θελφούσιοι, 1181 B 34, and Θελπούσιοι on coins (cf. Paus. VIII, 25, 2) is probably purely local. Θέλφουσα is Delphic (Wescher-Foucart, 464, 465) ; Τέλφουσα occurs in Polybius, II, 54, etc. Cf. G. Meyer, Gramm.[2] § 206.

ARCADIAN, DORIC, IONIC.

√ϝισ<ϝες in ϝιστίαν, see p. 89 , where the Thessalian and Boeotian forms are also adduced.

The form υἱύς (No. 1183, before 403) is probably pan-Hellenic, as it appears in Homer (υἱέος) and elsewhere chiefly in Doric inscrip-

---

[1] εἰ with the future in legal documents is foreign at least to Attic usage.

tions (Gortyn, υἱύς, IX, 40 ; Lacon. υἱύς, I. G. A. 54 ; Syracuse, ὑέεσσι) ; but also in Attic ὑύς C. I. A., I, 398₄, fifth century B.C.[1] υἱός appears, however, on one of the earliest Arcadian inscriptions, 1200₃ ('450 B.C.), and in Cyprian υἰῶ, 41. In Attic υἱός is found in a poetical inscription as early as 527–510 B.C.

The τρι- of Τρίτιος, 1203₈, is Indo-European, as also the τερ- of Aeolic τέρτος in Τερτικώνειος and τέρτα · ἡ τρίτη ; Boeotian τρίτος. Τέταρτος, 1249₈ ; Doric, Ionic, Attic τέταρτος as Homeric (also τέτρατος) ; Aeolic, τετραβαρήων ; Boeot. πέτρατος. Nothing can be gained from any attempt at a separation of the dialects into those that have αρ and those that have ρα from ερ. Cf. Brugmann, Grundriss, § 292.

ARCADIAN, AEOLIC, DORIC, AND IONIC-ATTIC.

ἐσλός, 1200 (about 450 B.C.). Cf. Sappho, 28 ; Ionic, I. G. A. 382₁ ; Doric according to Greg. Corinth, 213 ; Ahrens, 112. Not attested in Cyprian.

Arcad. ἐσδοκά ; Aeolic, Doric, δέκομαι ; Attic, δωροδόκος, πάνδοκος. δέχομαι is from δέξομαι, as βρέχω from βρέξω. Not attested in Cyprian.

Dative in -σι preceded by a vowel (-εσι). Arcad. ἐσδόσεσι, 1222₁₈ ; unattested in Cyprian. Homeric ἐπάλξεσιν, Attic, Cretan πόλεσι, all from assumed -ε stems.

PECULIARITIES OF ARCADIAN.

This section aims at collecting such Arcadisms as have not found entrance into the preceding paragraphs. In it are collected forms that have no precise parallel in other dialects as regard the word in question, or forms that embody phonetic changes occurring but rarely or even nowhere else in Hellas.

1. Fondness for the dental sonant as the representative of ϙ before ε.

NOTE. — The Doric dialects generally prefer δ before an open vowel, *e.g.* Delphic, Tarentinian, Cretan, Megarian, ὀδελός; whereas Boeotian and Homeric (Aeolic?) have ὀβελός. Attic has β before both ε and ο (διωβελία, ὀβελός, C. I. A., IV, 3, c, 5, and ὀβολός). Arcadian stands alone in having both δ and ζ for ϙ. It cannot be shown, however, that the rise of δ and ζ for ϙ took place on Peloponnesian soil alone. There is no proof whatsoever of the assumption that Doric forced δ into Arcadian, and thereby expelled "Aeolic" β, or that Doric caused Cyprian ζὰ, ἀζαθός.

---

[1] The old inflection maintained its ground in Attic till 350 B.C.

δέρεθρον and ζέρεθρα = Attic βάραθρον, βάραθρα ; Homeric βέρεθρον, Θ 14, Aeolic according to Hinrichs, De Hom. eloc. vest. Aeol.,
p. 62. These forms are found nowhere outside of Arcadian. ἐπιζαρέω,
Arcadian according to Eust. 909, 27, occurs also in Euripides. There
is no case of ἐπιβάρεω.

δέλλω and ζέλλω = βάλλω in Arcadian alone : ἐσδέλλοντες, 1222₄₉ ;
ζέλλειν · βάλλειν ; ἔζελεν · ἔβαλεν ; κάζελε · κατέβαλε. The variation
between δ and ζ in this and in the previous word indicates in all
probability a μετάπτωσις within the confines of Arcadia.[1]

The forms with ζ appear to be Tegean alone. This δ=ζ is different
from δ = I.E. *d.* Before the separation into dialects Greek did not
confound γε- and δε-. Cf. Cypr. σίς = τις, p. 117. The Arcadian
ζ = δ is found only where the β form prevails in other dialects.
Where a Cyprian ζ appears as a dialectic sound, it is the representative of γ in other dialects. There appears to be no connection between this ζ and that of Boeotian and Elean, whether or not the
latter was = *th'.*

2. ρ for λ in Κραριῶται πολῖται, 1231 (for Κλαρεῶται by dissimula-
tion, Brugmann, Grundriss, § 266 ; see Gelbke, p. 18 ; below, p. 109.
Bechtel compares Attic ναυκράρος, which, however, is not connected
according to G. Meyer, Curt. Stud. VII, 178. Cypr. Κλαριτά[ων?],
178, is probably connected with the river Κλάριος, near Soloi on
Cyprus. The interchange of λ and ρ can scarcely be elevated into
a distinguishing mark of agreement or difference between dialects.

3. δαρχμαί, 1222₂₃,₃₀, as in Elean ; in other dialects, δραχμαί ; δαρχ-
is not older than δραχ-, as both are from *r.* Cf. τέταρτος, p. 102.

4. Gen. sing. Ᾱ decl. fem. in -αυ from analogy to the masculine,
which has -αυ in both Arcadian and Cyprian. ζαμίαν from *ζαμίαο,
as Ἀπολλωνίδαυ ; οἰκίαν from *οἰκιᾱο (ϝιστίαν), etc. ; cf. p. 65. The
fem. article is always τᾶς, there being no starting-point for a *ταῦ.
See Leskien, Declination, p. 40 ; Osthoff, M. U., II, 128 ; Wilamowitz,
Zeitsch. für Gym. Wesen., 1877, p. 13.

6. Dative sing. -ες stems. Arcadian has the younger form in
πλήθι, 1222₂₀. Cf. also ἱράναι, the sole example, together with πλήθι,
of itacism in the Arcadian inscriptions, which have ει for ε. Cyprian has ει : ἔλει, 60₉ ; ϝέτει, 59₁. The contraction of ε(σ)ι to ῑ

---

[1] Cf. also πέζα for πέδα, according to Zenodotus both Doric and Arcadian. It
is at best a doubtful form. The ζ of ζέλλω ζέρεθρα must be distinguished from
Aeolic ζ = δι in ζά, Sappho 87 (ζάδηλος Alc. 18) and from the Cyprian ζ in
κόρζα = Aeolic κάρζα for καρδία (also Aeolic, Sappho, II, 6).

is extremely rare in the Greek dialects. See my paper on ει, ῑ, A. J. P. VI, No. 4.

7. Infinitive ἦναι, half-Doric, half-Ionic; see p. 69.

8. σφείς, 1222₁₀, accus. pl. (see passage quoted on p. 99). The form is certainly not Attic, since it is not used in a reflexive sense. All attempts to show the genesis of the form from *σφειες by a contraction of ιε to ι are fruitless, until such a phonetic change is well attested for Greek.

9. ἀπυδόας, 1222₁₈, is a form that has baffled explanation. Curt. Verb.² II, 314, thinks it is for *ἀπο-δό(σ)ας from *ἔδοα, after the pattern of ἔκηα, ἔχευα, εἶπα; and so Beermann, in Curt. Stud. IX, 78. Aorists without σ are found in inscriptions from Elis, Argos, Sparta, and in late Cyprian. Spitzer thinks ἀποδόᾱς stands for *ἀπυδοανς < ἀπυδοαντς, comparing τός < τόνς.

NOTE. — Cyprian has apparently a modification of √δω in δυϝάνοι, if a different root is not at the base of this remarkable form. See p. 114.

10. -δε for -δα in θύρδα· ἔξω· Ἀρκάδες.

11. -τοι for -ται, perhaps from analogy to -το; cf. Thess. -τει, and p. 86.

12. ἐφθορκώς, 1222₁₀, contains the regular ablaut form of ερ, the oρ here not being the so-called Aeolic equivalent of ρα or αρ.[1] Curtius was the first to call special attention to the love of "dark" vowels in dialects connected with Aeolic (Bemerkungen zur gr. Dialektologie Gött. Nachr., 1862 = Kleine Schriften, pp. 156, 157). Since his time this has been held as a criterion of the connection of Boeotian (Καλλίστροτος, πόρνοψ), Thessalian (στροταγέντος, κόρνοψ), and Cyprian (κόρζα = καρδία). But it is probable that to this assumed mint-mark of Aeolism too much importance has been attached. Thus τέτορθαι and μέμορθαι contain, as does pan-Hellenic ἔπορον, the regular ablaut form of ερ.[2] ἀστροπά = Attic στραπή may contain the ablaut of √στερπ, etc. No investigation of sufficient thoroughness dealing with the dialect appearances of oρ, ρο : αρ, ρα has as yet been instituted from this point of view. If oρ or ρο is Aeolic for αρ or ρα, it cannot have been a phonetic change called into being by the operation of a law that necessitated an oρ or ρο in every weak form. Thus we have Cyprian κόρζα, but Aeolic κάρζα and καρδίαν. Or, if this be nevertheless maintained, the result is that Arcadian[3] and Thessalian

---

[1] See Spitzer, p. 12.

[2] Brugmann, Grundriss, § 292, holds to their Aeolic character.

[3] Neither στρατο- nor στροτο- is preserved in the Cyprian.

στρατο-, by the side of Aeolic στροτάγω and Boeotian ἐστροτεύαθη, must be explained as loan formations from Doric. Or the law must have been so overcome by forces of analogy, and at so early date, that it is no " law" at all. See Tarbell's paper on Phonetic Law, in the Transactions, Vol. XVII, p. 10.

> NOTE. — That the dialects of non-Aeolic coloring present examples of ορ for the weak αρ, where the "Aeolic" dialects have αρ, *e.g.* Arcad. γραφής, shows that this assumed Aeolic peculiarity often fails at a critical point. Cf. Doric τέτοοες; Meg. Argol. γραφ-; Arcad. γραφής.[1] Where ορ may be the regular strong form of ερ, then the "Aeolic" dialects fall into line. Only with the widest latitude may we assume that Aeolic in the strict sense, Thessalian, Boeotian, Arcadian, and Cyprian have a predilection for the "dark" vowel ο.

13. ο for α occurs also in ἑκοτόν in Ἐκοτόμβοια, 1222₂₃; Ἐκοτόν-βοια, 1232₉. No other dialect except Arcadian has this form. ἑκο-τόν is not to be regarded as an example of an "Aeolic" love of ο in place of α, since that conclusion rests upon a mere external compari-son of the Arcadian and the common form. As δεκόταν, 1198, owes its ο to the ο of -κοντα, so, too, does ἑκοτόν. It is noticeable to ob-serve the conflict of tendencies within the limits of a single dialect. δεκόταν and ἑκοτόν have both fallen under the sway of the frequently recurring -κοντα; yet τριακάσιοι, which stood in closer touch with -κοντα, has maintained its ancient vocalism, though Ionic, Attic, and Aeolic have permitted the corresponding word to be swept along with the current of analogy. Cf. Spitzer, p. 11.

We now pass to an attempt at displaying the points of divergence between Arcadian and Cyprian from the Cyprian point of view. It may be impossible to prove that in possess-ing a certain form, or in giving scope to a certain phonetic law, Cyprian may have deviated from the Arcado-Cyprian norm. The deviation may have been Arcadian, and not Cy-prian. The age of the monuments is too late to permit us definitely to ascribe to Arcado-Cyprian a form which in Cy-prian differs from Arcadian, and which is preserved upon an Arcadian inscription older than the Cyprian one in question. Furthermore, the paucity of materials in each dialect is sin-gularly noticeable. At the present day we have but about nine hundred words preserved to us in Arcadian, and but

---

[1] Elean has both γροφ- and γραφ-, the latter more frequently. Cf. also El. κοθάρσι, Locr. περϞοθαριὰν.

about five hundred in Cyprian, inscriptions. On the age of the few older Arcadian inscriptions, see Roberts, § 107. The wide universality of their interrelations with dialects of variant types is too great to permit conclusions as to the existence or non-existence of any given form in either of the dialects.

CYPRIAN AND AEOLIC.

1. μ for β in κυμερῆναι, 68; cf. Et. Mag. 543₂; Et. Gud. 351₉. κυβερνήτης· ἀναλόγως οἱ Αἰολεῖς κυμερνήτην λέγουσιν. κυμερῆναι with Ionic -ναι (on Arcado-Cyprian Homeric -ναι, see p. 69) from *κυμερέω or *κυμεράω, parallel form to κυβερνάω.[1] Deecke (B. B., VI, 81) compares Cyprian Τρεμιθοῦς from τρέμιθος = τερέβινθος. This word and others (*e.g.* Aeolic βάρμιτον = βάρβιτον[2]), containing a supposed interchange of μ and β, are all uncertain. The certain interrelation of μ and β is, however, not confined solely to Cyprian and to Aeolic, as it comes to light in Rhodian περιβολιβῶσαι (Cauer,[2] 176₁₀), and (chiefly) in Hesychian glosses (G. Meyer, Gramm.[2] § 180).

In ἱρῶνι, 60₈, we have the contraction of ιε to be observed in Aeolic ἴρος (if not, as is probable, from ἰσρ-, according to Osthoff, M. U., IV, 149). Cyprian has also ἱερός and ἱαρός, though the latter form is not so well attested. Arcadian, too, has both forms. A supposed contraction of ιε to ῑ in Aeolic and Cyprian has no bearing on an Arcado-Cyprian connection with Aeolic, since ἱρός is also Ionic (Homer, exclusively in Herodotean usage, Thasos, Cauer,[2] 527₉).

Several points of supposed connection between Cyprian and Aeolic may here be briefly alluded to.

ἔκερσε, 32; cf. N 546, K 456, Aspis 419, and in Aeschylus. For a list of aorists with ρς and λς, see Curt. Verb.[2] II, 299. Similar formations in the future are called Aeolic by the grammarians (quoted Meister, Dialekte, I, p. 182) on account of their barytone character, but for no cogent reason whatever.

The Aeolic form is πέντε, not πέμπε, as has long been assumed (see Meister, in Studia Nicolaitana, p. 10). Neither the Cyprian

---

[1] Ground forms are (1) kʷmér = κυμερ-, κυμερῆναι; (2) kʷmr- = κυβρ-, κυβαρ-. From kʷbr̥ + na + en = κυβαρνᾶν. κυβερ- received its ερ from κυμερ-. On -mr- or -mr̥- yielding -βρ-, -βαρ- (and not -μβρ-) in the middle of a word, see Johansson, De derivatis verbis contractis, p. 59.

[2] Quoted by Ahrens, I, p. 45, together with κυμερνήτης as a doubtful example of an Aeolic change of β to μ.

πε(μ)φαμέρων¹ (gen. sing.) nor the Alcaean πέμπων (33) presupposes πέμπε, since *πενq- stands before a dark vowel, as in Homeric πεμπώβολον. There is no need to correct Sappho's πεντεβόηα (frag. 98), or to regard any form with πεντ- as borrowed from the κοινή (πεντάμναιον, Coll. 276). πέντε is pan-Hellenic, and τ prevailed originally in all dialects before ε; later on, forms like πεντώβολος and πεντάς came into existence from a confusion with π- forms (πεμπάς, etc.), in the same manner as π in πέσσαρες, πείσει, took the place of τ.

Cyprian and Aeolic have ζ for δι- of other dialects, when the accent did not fall originally on the syllable with ι. Aeolic ζά-, κάρζα ; Paphian κόρζα ; Arcadian διακωλύοι and δι- in every case.

CYPRIAN AND THESSALIAN.

A remarkable case of similarity between Cyprian and Thessalian is found in Cyprian, πείσει, 60₁₂,₂₅ ; Thessal. πεισάτου = τεισάτω. Arcadian has here ἀπυτειέτω, 1222₄₃ ; ἀπυτεισάτω, 1222₃₅ : cf. ἔστεισιν, 1222₃₇ ; Τείσανδρος, 1234 ; Τείσιμος, 1247 ; Τεισιμάχ[ω], 1247 ; as Locrian, Cretan, ἀποτείσει ; Heracl. ἀποτεισεῖ ; old Attic, ἀπο]τεῖσαι ; Delphic, προτέτεικεν. The Cyprian and Thessalian form is later as regards the labial instead of the dental before ει, since π of πείσει was taken from that of ποινή and *πέποιqα after the separation of Cyprian and Arcadian. The Thessalian form only proves that a similar phonetic levelling can take place in two dialects without the influence of one upon the other. Thessalian πεισάτου came into existence after all immediate connection between Thessalian and Aeolic or Boeotian had ceased. It is absurd with Brand (p. 62) to postulate a pan-Aeolic πει-, or to assume a pan-Aeolic preference for labial sounds where the older dialects have dentals or gutturals.

A further example of parallelism between the dialects in the field of palatal sounds is doubtful. : Thessal. κίς = τίς, but κέ = τέ in Cyprian is open to grave suspicion. See Deecke in Bezzenberger's Beiträge, VIII, 153; Brugmann in Techmer's Zeitschrift für allg. Sprachw., I, 233.

No immediate connection between Cyprian and Thessalian can be maintained on the score of the accusatives, ἀ(ν)δριγά(ν)ταν, 59 ; ἰυατῆραν, 60₃. The Larissaean inscription, 1332₄₀, has κιόναν from κιών. This analogical formation on the lines of the Ā declension occurs in Cratylus, 404 B, Δήμητραν (Schanz, Δήμητρα), and in the epigraphic

---

¹ So Deecke; G. Meyer, πε(μ)πάμερων.

forms in Kaibel: πατέραν, 372 ; μητέραν, 522 ; λιμέναν, 168 Thessaly ; νεότηταν, 368 ; πατρίδαν, 920 ; ἄνδραν, C. I. G. 1781, Thessaly. According to Franz, ἀνδρειάνταν, according to Kaibel (No. 406), ἀνδρειάντ'. Cf. Sturz, De dialecto Macedonica, p. 127. The Cyprian forms quoted above are in general older than those adduced from Kaibel and the Corpus according to Wagner (Quaest. de epigram., p. 107).

Ahrens (Philol. XXXV, 13) and Neubauer (Comm. phil. in honor. Mommseni p. 280), are in error in regarding Thessalian and Cyprian on a plane in the possession of the rarer form of the name of Apollo. See above, p. 97. Thessalian Ἄπλουν (= Ἄπλων) is certain, but Ἀπόλ(λ)ων is in every case the Cyprian form according to the transcribers, though the other form is not impossible. See Bezzenberger's Beiträge, IX, 328.

Curtius held that the Cyprians and Thessalians changed ω to ου. Of the examples that he quotes, Ἄπλουν does not exist in Cyprian, and ἐρουά = ἐρωή (cf. ἀλουᾶ· κήπῳ = Hom. ἀλωῇ) cannot be regarded as an example of that ου which in Thessalian has supplanted every case of ω. ω in the Cyprian inscriptions never becomes ου.

CYPRIAN, AEOLIC, THESSALIAN.

Infinitive in -ην.

The Cyprian form *e·ke·ne*, 60₁₀, has been differently transcribed. The -εν of Arcadian has led some to claim that the Cyprian form is ἔχεν, and hence of Doric coloring ; but Deecke now writes ἔχην. -ην is exceedingly frequent in Aeolic even in the aorist passive, and in the Pharsalian idiom we have ἔχειν, which is for ἔχην. Thess. ει = η. The other divisions of Thessaly have -μεν. The Elean form is likewise -ην, according to Blass, Coll. 1153, 1156.

ὀν = ἀνά has already been referred to, p. 88.

CYPRIAN AND BOEOTIAN.

The genitive in -ᾱο (Homeric and Boeotian) is exceptional in Cyprian, *e.g.* Κυπραγόραο, 79 ; Δαγατίσαο, 58. Arcadian and Cyprian have generally -αυ. Forms like Σωκλείδα in Boeotian are very rare, as in Cypr., cf. Ἀμηνίγα, 60₁₈.

Ὕϝηι, 124, from Ὕεύς (or Ὕης?). This agrees with the Boeot. ending ευ < ηι (*e.g.* Φωκεῦ). ηι from ηυ stems is Homeric, Ionic, Attic, Doric -ει, and never ηι.

Cyprian, Boeotian, (and Doric) proper names in -ιᾱς for -εᾱς are not infrequent. A certain explanation of their interrelation has, however, not yet been given.

CYPRIAN, AEOLIC, AND BOEOTIAN.

α + ε = η in Doric, North Greek, and perhaps in Elean. In Cyprian, Aeolic, Boeotian, and Ionic, the result of the contraction is ᾱ. Johansson, p. 58, is doubtful whether there was not an Arcado-Cyprian contraction of α + ε to η. We have no certain example in Arcadian. Johansson explains ἰδίπα, Coll. 49, by the suggestion that Cyprian, after its separation from Arcadian, may have adopted vowel contractions different from those prevalent in the Arcado-Cyprian period. ἰγᾶσθαι, 60₈, is also cited by Johansson as a possible example of the later contraction. But neither Johansson nor Spitzer has any right to suppose *a priori* that Arcadian would agree with Doric in contracting α + ε to η. Furthermore, Hall, Rev. A. O. S., XI, 217, says that Deecke's transcription of No. •49 is nearly all wrong. He himself reads . . . *pa· ti· sa· to· ro.*

ϝρ- occurs in Cyprian, Aeolic (gramm.), Boeotian, and in Elean. It does not appear on any Doric monument.

CYPRIAN, BOEOTIAN, THESSALIAN.

Arcadian and Elean do not change ε to ι before vowels, though ἐν + consonant has become ἰν.[1] In Cyprian the change is well attested : ἀτελίγα, 60₂₃; ἰό(ν)τα, 60₂₃; ἐπιό(ν)τα, 60₁₉; κατέθιγαν, 60₂₇; θιῷ, 37 (θεῷ, 27). In fact, every ε before α or ο becomes ι, except when ϝ has disappeared between ε and ο, *e.g.* ἱερέος, or where -εος is from ε(σ)ος, nom. -ης, *e.g.* Τιμοκλέϝεος and in Τιμοκρέτεος, Φιλοκρέτεος, Berl. Phil. Wochenschr., 1886, p. 1291. κατέθισαν in No. 20, if for *κατέθεσαν, would offer the sole exception to the rule that ε becomes ι in Cyprian only before a vowel.[2] Deecke's reading, which he himself finds remarkable on account of the preservation of the intervocalic σ (Zweiter Nachtrag in B. B., VIII), must therefore yield

---

[1] Κραριῶται, 1231, B 35, etc., is referred by Gelbke, p. 18, to Doric influence. Instances of ε are ἐόντος, 1222₁₁; Ἀντιφάεος, 1231, C 7; Ξενοφάνεος, 1231, C 21; Ξενοκράτεος, 1248₅. Ἀγαθίας by the side of Ἀγασέας is of course not a case of change of ε to ι.

[2] ϝιστίαυ, Arcad. 1203₁₈, seems to offer some contradiction. But ε + s + cons. may become ι in all dialects. Lesbian and Attic alone have ἑστία; Hom., Ion., Locr., Boeot., Cret., Heracl., have ἱστ-.

to κατέθιγαν, as the sign *sa ·* is not far removed from that for *ya ·* Johansson (Några ord, etc., p. 31) assumes κατέθιγαν<κατέθιαν<κατέθισαν.

The Cyprian dialect in its substitution of ι for ε before a vowel is on a plane with Boeotian (the chief seat of the change), Thessalian (except in the inscription from Larissa), and with Doric to a limited degree, viz., especially in -εω verbs, θεός, κλέος, πλέων, forms of -ες stems, etc. (Laconian, Messenian, Cretan, Argolic, Heraclean). In Aeolic the supposed change of ε to ι is limited to words like χρύσιος, χάλκιος, μαρμάριος, which lend themselves to a different explanation as regards the ι, and in the gen. γλύκιος ; cf. p. 84.

The difference in the treatment of antevocalic ε is one of the most noticeable mint-marks distinguishing Arcadian from Cyprian. The Arcadian type has remained true to an Arcado-Cyprian preservation of antevocalic ε. The ι for ε must in any theory of a pan-Aeolic dialect be regarded as subsequent to the separation into sub-dialects. Wherever the substitution of ι for ε occurs, it is to be regarded as the effect of a tendency obtaining to a greater or less degree throughout Greece, and is merely more prevalent in the dialects of the "Aeolic" type. Even in old Attic we have Αἰνιᾶται, Αὐλιᾶται. In Ionic the change is expressed by ει (εἰαυτόν, ἐννεία). In Boeotian and Ionic-Attic the ε remained a closed ε : Boeot. ε, ει, ι ; Ionic-Attic, ε, ει.

CYPRIAN, AEOLIC, THESSALIAN, BOEOTIAN.

Absence of ν ἐφελκυστικόν from all prose non-κοινή inscriptions is the only feature common to these four dialects.[1] The Arcadian dialect has [ἀνέ]θηκε[ν], according to Bechtel (No. 1218) ; ἀνέ[θ]ηκεν in an epigram (Roberts, No. 280) is an epic reminiscence. All other cases of this verbal form occur at the end of the inscriptions and have no -ν. ἔδοξεν (1183$_{1,6}$ = Roberts, 283) is the only certain case of ν in a verbal form, and that in the inscription containing Ἀλειοῖσι (p. 84). Roberts, p. 281, holds that Alea is referred to. No. 1183, it should be remarked, was found at Olympia, but Elean has no paragogic ν. -ν in ἀναλώμασιν μή, 1222$_{41}$, is the only example in noun formations in Arcadian.

Whether the presence of -ν in these two forms is to be ascribed to Laconian influence is doubtful. In the oldest Spartan inscriptions it

---

[1] A recently discovered Cyprian example is: ἔστασε Ἄριστος, Berl. Phil. Wochens., 1886, p. 1291. But the Tarmassus inscription has ἔδωκεν, ὀνέθηκεν, the only examples in Cyprian ; l. l., 1886, p. 1323.

is not present, but as it is frequent in those of later date, and in the Heraclean tablets, the possibility of Doric influence here cannot be authoritatively denied.

CYPRIAN, IONIC-ATTIC.

There is no case of η for ᾱ, except, perhaps, Ἰαλεφήμω, Hall, Rev. A. O. S., XI, 234.

πρωτωτίμω contains the contraction of o + a to ω. Aeolic examples of πρῶτος are now generally ascribed to the influence of Hellenistic scribes or stone-cutters. Neither πρῶτος nor πρᾶτος occurs in Arcadian. The latter form is that to be expected.

Ἀμύ(ν)τω, 41, and Εὐφαγόρω, 153, 154 (410–374 B.C.), are referred by Meyer, Gramm.[2] § 345, to Ionic influence. This is, perhaps, better than to regard them as drawn over to the O declension in the same fashion as Homeric ἠΰκομος from κόμη, and ἐϋμμελίω from μελία. Cf. Fick, Odyssee, p. 325.

On a + ε = ᾱ in Cyprian, see above, p. 81, and on -ηι in -ηυ-stems, see above, p. 108.

Cyprian ὅτε, πότε as in Ionic-Attic. Aeolic ὅτα, Doric πόκα, Elean τόκα, Pamphyl. ὅκα, Abu-Simb. ὅκα. We do not know whether Arcadian μεστ᾿ is for μέστα or μέστε. Brand's assumption (p. 34) that the Cyprian forms in τε are descended from a pan-Aeolic τα is certainly wide of the mark, as they represent the original -qe. The Aeolic τα is itself later than either -τε or -κα.

ἀρούραι, 60₂₀ (a · ro · u · ra · i ·), implies the existence of a genuine diphthong ov; and this is assumed by Fick (Odyssee, p. 324) ; cf. Leo Meyer, Gramm.[2] p. 674. But if we compare ἀρO[ρ]ηι, I. G. A. 497, b. 17 (Teos), the parallel forms to Ionic ἀρούρη in Doric and Aeolic would be ἀρώρα[1] and ἄρορρα. It must be confessed that the etymology of ἀρούρα is too uncertain to permit the statement that we have here a loan form from Ionic. ὅρα as extracted from ἐσόρα · ὄπισθεν, which is claimed by Rothe to be Paphian (for οὐρά, *tail*), has a very shadowy existence. To further complicate matters, we have a Miletan ὡρή = οὐρά (Revue archéol., 1874, p. 100). ἀρούρ[ας] occurs on a Thessalian inscription, Coll. No. 371. Rutherford, Phrynichus, p. 14, incorrectly calls ἀρούρα for γῆ old Ionic and poetic. See A. J. P. VIII, 469.

With the frequent names in Ὀνα- (Ὀναίων, Ὄνασις, Ὀνάσιλος, etc.), cf. the Ionic ὀνήϊστος (ὄναιον · ἄρειον).

---

[1] ἀρωραῖοι, Acharnians, 762, was expelled by Ahrens, who adopted the reading of the Rav., ἀρουραῖοι.

CYPRIAN AND DORIC.

1. Compensatory lengthening in τώς (but see p. 86) and in ἠμί in twenty cases; in one of these, No. 93, Voigt reads ἐμ(μ)ι Σηθικᾶ, following Neubauer's transcription. The transcribers, however, have generally decided against the Aeolic and Thessalian form; and Hall, Rev. A. O. S., XI, 228, accepts ἠμί here as elsewhere.

2. Contraction of εο to ω in Νωμηνίων = Νουμηνίον, cf. νεϝοστάτας, 59₂ (Berl. Phil. Wochens., 1886, p. 1323), and in σπέως, 31, 32, if Deecke's reading be correct. I would prefer σπήως, from *σπέϝεσος. ω < εο is found on Doric soil in Cretan monuments alone: παρακαλώμενα, εὐχαριτῶμες. εο in Aeolic = εο, ευ, (Ionic influence?) never ω. ε + ο in Arcado-Cyprian remain uncontracted in gen. sing. of -ης stems. ε remains before ο and ω in Arcadian in Κλεονόμω, Θεοτέλεος.

3. The Doric genitive in ᾱ (if the α does not, as Deecke claims, represent αυ) is found in 'Αμηνίγα, 60₁₈, 'Ονασιμάλα, 120. The Ζωτέα of Deecke, No. 77, is read by Hall, Ζωτή[ς]. Ζωτέα occurs, No. 122, apparently as a genitive. 'Αριστίγα, Berl. Phil. Wochens., 1886, p. 1643.

4. On Cyprian ποῖ, see p. 67.

5. Expulsion of secondary, intervocalic σ is foreign to Arcadian, but occurs in Cyprian, Laconian, Elean, and Argolic. The examples are διμώοις, 69 = διμούσοις and φρονέωι, 68, which should be φρονίγωι, or, at least in certain parts of the island (Chytrea), φρονίωι. The subjunctive is here used without κέ (ἄν does not occur), as in Homer and elsewhere in relative sentences. This is the first epigraphic example of the secondary loss of σ, a phenomenon attested by Hesychian glosses, ἴμαόν· πάταξον, ἰμπάταόν· ἔμβλεψον, etc. (M. Schmidt, in K. Z., IX, 367). In all other cases, intervocalic σ is preserved intact in Cyprian: κατέστασε, λῦσαι, λύση. Cf. Laconian ἐποίηέ, I. G. A. 80, Elean ποήασσαι = ποιήσασθαι, Argolic ἐποίϝηέ, I. G. A. 42. The Cyprian forms without the σ are only apparent survivals of the period in which σ disappeared regularly between vowels in the aorist, and not, as Osthoff maintains, a residuum of that period. See Müller, De Σ inter vocales posita, pp. 80, 81. In his Kleine Schriften, II, 152, Curtius suggests that the loss of σ in Laconian is due to dialect mixture.

CYPRIAN-AEOLIC, DORIC, IONIC, ATTIC.

-ην is accusative of -ες stems: ἀτελῆν, 60₁₀. This analogical phenomenon, though not occurring in every dialect in Greece, is sufficiently general to be recognized as a universal feature of Greek morphology. As a rule, the influence of the Â declension makes itself apparent only in the later period of the development of the language, though it comes to light as early as the time of Homer (ζαῆν or ζάην). Attic Σωκράτην, Ionic Λυσικλῆν, Cretan Ἱεροκλῆν, Boeot. Διογένειν, Aeolic δαμοτέλην.[1] Arcadian has no similar metaplastic accusative. Wagner, Quaest. gramm. de epigrammatis, pp. 107, 108, has collected the examples from Kaibel's Epigrammata, embracing forms from Halicarnassus, Sardis, Athens, and Thebes. Tauromenium and Pamphylia have -ην in the adjectival flexion.

PECULIARITIES OF CYPRIAN.

In this section a list of some of the chief peculiarities of the Cyprian epigraphic forms has been attempted, and explanations given when possible. Rothe's Quaestiones de Cypriorum dialecto et vetere et recentiore has never progressed beyond a partial examination of the vowel relations of the Cyprian glosses.

I. Vowels.

ἐρ in Hesychian glosses: κατ' ἐρ' ἔζεαι· κάθισαι, Πάφιοι. κατ' ἐρ' ἔζεο· κατέζου. κατ' ἐρ' ἔζετο· ἐκαθίζετο.[2] G. Meyer, Gramm.² § 55, regards ἐρ (without the apostrophe) as the strong form of ἄρα, ἄρ, ῥά. Spitzer, pp. 7, 8, holds that ἔρα may be a contamination of *ἔρ and ἄρα. Cf. Bloomfield, A. J. P., VI, 44 ff.; Brugmann, Berichte der Sächsisch. Gesell. der Wissensch., 1883, p. 37 ff. With this strong form compare -κρέτης and p. 90. This gloss is apparently derived from a text of Homer in vogue in Cyprus (probably not ἡ Κυπρία). On the Arcadian form ἄρ or ἄρ', see Roberts, No. 277, and above, p. 80.

In τέρχνιγα, 60₉, 18-19, 22 compared with τρέχνος and τέρχνεα (Hesychius), we have an instance of metathesis without vowel-lengthening that appears to be restricted to no particular dialect. If ταρχάνιον·

[1] Analogy of Â stems: Genitive -ου in Attic, Delphic, Cnidos, Thasos, Scyros, etc.; gen. in η in Aeolic alone. Dat. ῃ in Aeolic. Voc. in η, Arcadian, p. 99.
[2] Curtius held ἐρ to be Arcadian. But I find this unattested.

ἐντάφιον and τέρχνεα· ἐντάφια (besides φυτὰ νέα) do not contain a confusion of two separate words, τέρχνεα is another example of the Cyprian fondness for ερ.

In Σελαμινί[ων, 176, 177, and Berl. Phil. Wochenschr., 1886, p. 1291, compared with Σαλαμίνιος, 148, we have an interchange of ε and α which cannot be controlled by any known parallels in Cyprian. Deecke suggests that Σελ- recalls the Assyrian form of the name of the city of Silhimi, and is evidence in favor of Semetic influence (Josephus mentions a Σελαμίν in Galilaea). But Dr. Hall has suggested to me that the ε may be an orthographical slip. Its appearance is too extensive to assume this with certainty. In any case, it is unwise to deduce from its appearance any such far-reaching conclusion as that of Deecke.

The relation of ω to υ in δυϝάνοι, 60₆ = διδοίη, is not established. δώκοι occurs 60₁₆. δυϝάνοι shows that the υ from υ υ had not become extinct; Brugmann, Grundriss, § 166. Cf. also Chalc. Γαρυϝόνης. On the assumed change of ω to ου in Cyprian, see p. 108. Rothe, p. 72, finds no certain case of ω for υ in the glosses.

αἴλων (= ἄλλων), 60₁₄; cf. Arcad. ἄλλοις and ἄλλος in all other Greek dialects. αἰλότερον· ἀλλοιότροπον occurs in Hesychius, who, however, names no source. In Et. Mag. 34₁₀, for αἶλα, ἀντὶ τοῦ καλὰ Κύπριοι, read ἀντὶ τοῦ ἄλλα.

An Elean αἶλος cannot be upheld, since in ΑΙΛΟΤΡΙΑ, 1154₂ (an exceedingly corrupt inscription) I is, according to Blass, *entweder zu streichen (Roehl) oder in Λ zu corrigieren (die Inschrift hat freilich keine Verdoppelung).* ἄλλοιρ occurs in Elean, 1172; cf. τἆλλα, 1152. Cyprian seems here to have bifurcated from Arcadian in choosing a form that preserves, though in the tonic syllable, the ι, which was the cause of the geminated liquid of every other dialect. But instead of the genealogical tree commonly adopted and vigorously defended by Meinck, De epenthesis graeca, p. 41,

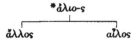

we must assume that the original Cyprian form was not different from the Arcadian, and that αιλ is merely a secondary development from αλλ. See Spitzer, p. 34, and Weinhold, Alleman. gram., 138; Baier. gram., p. 183.[1] Cases of mouillization which might be adduced

---

[1] It would at least be extremely hazardous to deny on the score of this form alone that ἄλλος was formed from ἀλιος before the separation of the parent Greek

from the Romance languages (Fr. ail, It. aglio>allium ; merveille, meraviglia>mirabilia ; meilleur, migliore>meliorem) are only apparent parallels, the presence of *i* after *l* being necessary in order that it be drawn into the tonic syllable. In the dialect of Crete, λ before a consonant was pronounced as *ḷ*, and as such is represented by *v* ; cf. αὐκά = ἀλκή, θεύγω = θέλγω. It is therefore not impossible that a somewhat similar affection may have formed an αλλος, which cannot then be regarded as an example of epenthesis.

It should not be suppressed that Brand (De dialectis Aeolicis, p. 50) has attempted on the strength of αλλος and αἰλότρια to formulate the law *a ante liquidam positum non in a longum sed in aι produxisse.* This cannot be accepted, nor can his explanation that χαίρω, μέλαινα result from compensatory lengthening, and not from epenthesis.

αυ in *ἀμαύω in Νοσταμαύσα[ντος], Deecke, B. B., IX, 251 ; cf. ἀμεύω, ἀμευσίπορος.

ϝήπω μέγα in 68 is regarded as an aorist, not as a present by Deecke, who translates : *Ein grosses will ich verkunden.* Hall, in his review of Deecke's collection (A. O. S., XI, 220), holds to the present : *I speak a great thing.* Deecke (Bezz. Beitr., VI, 79) rejects Ahrens' ϝέπω, and maintains that η for ει is regular in Cyprian. I cannot regard this as correct. εἶπον has the genuine diphthong ει, and as such is written with ΕΙ on pre-Euclidian Attic inscriptions (Meisterhans, p. 79) and on the monuments of other dialects (Smyth, Diphthong EI, pp. 57, 60).[1] The ει is therefore not the result of contraction (ἐϝέϝεπον), but from ε + ι (ἐϝέϝιπον). Priscian's (I, 54) so-called Aeolic ἦπον is a blunder for ἦπον, because the absence of ι ἀνεκφώνητον was regarded by the grammarians as a peculiarity of Aeolic (Meister., I, 71). Now there can be no question that in no period except the itacistic was genuine ει confounded with η > ε + ε in any Greek dialect ;[2] and that in Cyprian this should have been

into dialects. In Greek, epenthesis took place before the dialect period. The Cyprian 'Απείλωνι is, I conjecture, to be explained in like fashion with αλλος. That this is the only possible explanation for the ει form, occurred to me before reading Deecke's similar suggestion in the Berliner Philol. Wochenschrift, 1886, p. 217.

[1] On the Gortynian inscription, we have προϝΕΙπάτω, etc.

[2] This must hold good despite Arcado-Cyprian ἀμην- (Arcad. 'Αμηνέας; Cypr. 'Αμηνίγα: cf. Amorg. 'Αμείνον[ι], I. G. A. 390). Arcadian Πλησtίερος Πλειστίερος. C. I. G. has no case of Πληστ- except Πληστονείκα, 1506 (Sparta), with the ominous *ex schedis Fourmonti* : Πλειστονίκης, 1363, 1364 b, 2810 b, add., 2813. Cf. above, p. 93. Cypr. ἠ, "if," has been explained above, p. 72, as either = ἤ(ν) or as a separate form. It is not a Cyprian form of εἰ.

the case is incredible, and is in fact disproved by the diphthongal orthography *pe · i · se · i* = πείσει. Spurious ει became diphthongal in Attica about 380 B.C., but there is no proof that the sound resulting from the contraction of ε + ε (admitting for the moment that ἐϝέϝ:πον, or even ϝέϝεπον, was the source of εἶπον) — a sound different from that of the Attic spurious ει — ever became diphthongal in Cyprian.

In every case EI remains a genuine diphthong: αἰϝεί, ἐϝείσης, ἕλει, ἔτει, ϝέτει, εὐζαϝεῖτε, ϝεικόνα, πείσει.[1] In Arcadian genuine ει remains except in πλῆθι, ἱράναι. This shows, to my thinking, that whatever we may think of the characters *ve · po ·,* and however much we may be inclined to ascribe the η of ϝήπω to an irresolute orthography, a Cyprian change of genuine ει to η is not regular. Allusion has already been made above, p. 68, to the difficulties in the way of a satisfactory explanation of πότι, "lord," in the same line; and as regards the hexameters, which Deecke insists on to the discomfiture of Ahrens' ϝέπω, Hall remarks that they are not clear according to his more certain transliteration, the characters having gradually become plainer since the time the stone was exhumed.

II. Consonants.

ζ for γ in ἀζαθᾶι, 37, 59, and in ζᾶι = γᾶι; cf. Arcad. γᾶν, Doric δᾶ, Et. Mag. 60₈. The γ in the latter word is probably palatal, cf. Zend *zāo*, Lith. *žemè*, Slav. *zemlja*, K. Z., XXV, 146. Johansson in B. B. XIII, 117, has resurrected the old etymology, — Goth. *gods.* The substitution of ζ for γ in ἀζαθός may stand in connection with the spirant pronunciation of γ prevalent from the second century B.C. This, though exceedingly doubtful, is better than to regard the ζ as originating in like manner with the palatal spirants of the Aryan and Slavo-Lettic languages. See K. Z., XXV, 150.

NOTE 1. — Cypr. καλήζω is not necessarily a proof that ζ is a representative of *yod.*

NOTE 2. — ι between vowels was thickened to γ, or at least could be represented by γ in θέαγον = Ionic θεῄιον. Cf. Heracl. ποτικλαίγωσα.

In all dialects there was heard a parasitic glide sound between ι and a following vowel.[2] This sound assumes graphic expression, with the exception of Pamphylian, in Cyprian alone, but even there with

[1] ϝΕλεοδάμω, 117, is uncertain.

[2] In Boeotian ἀνέθειαν, ει represents a closed ε, and not ε + ι, a distinct glide sound. On the development of intervocalic ι in several dialects, *e.g.* Attic θειοῖν, εἰᾶν, etc., cf. above, p. 110.

no great consistency. Thus in the inscriptions from Dali it is found fifteen times, of which thirteen occur in No. 60,[1] two in No. 59.[2] It is not written in Γολγίαι in 61, nor in ἐπιό(ν)τα, 60 $_{9, 19, 22}$; ἰό(ν)τα, 60 $_{23}$; πανώνιον, 60 $_{10}$; πανωνίω, 60 $_{22}$: nor in Κετίων, 59; Κετιέϝες, 60 $_1$; ἀ(ν)- δριά(ν)ταν, Berl. Phil. Wochenschr., 1886, p. 1323; elsewhere always with *y*. From *Chytréa* we have no *yod* in Παφίας Παφίαι, 1, 4, 5, 6, 9, 10, 12, following Hall's corrections, nor any in ἰερῆϝος in No. 1. *Kerynia* has both Παφίγας, 15, and Παφίας, 16; *Palaeachora*, Στα- σίγαυ, 17, Στασίγας, 18, and no example of the omission; *Polis-tis- Chrysochou*, Ἀριστίγαν, 20, Berl. Phil. Wochenschr., 1886, p. 1643; and κατέθιγαν, 20 (see p. 109); but Ναστώταυ and Ὀναίων, 21 (for which Baunack reads Ὀναῖων). *Drimu* has Ἰολάω(?), 26; *Ktima*, ἰγερής, 33; *Kúklia*, ἰγερεύς, 40; ἰγερέος, 39; ἰγαρώτατος and ὁσέγα, 41; but δεξίωι, 37, and ἰερέος, 38. *Golgoi*, Διγαίθεμι, 74 (cf. Διϝείθεμις, 60 $_{21}$); Παφίγαν, 69; but Διάθεμι, 100; Διός, 73; εὐϝεργεσίας, 71; ϝλακανίω and Ἀφροδισίω, 86; Θεμίαν, 66, in Greek letters; Ὀνασίω- ρο, 75; Ἰαρώ(ν)δαυ, ᴘ18. *Abydos*, Σαλαμίνιος, 148; *Pyla*, Μαγιρίω, 120, 121 (Hall).

In the above-cited examples *yod* appears twenty-two times, and only four times before ε, seventeen times before α,[3] once before ι, and never before any other sound. In the other examples of the occur- rences of *yod*, α follows in almost every instance: Σκύγαρος, 33; Ἄγα- ρος, 31 (= Ἄϊρος?), *Ktima*; Δαγατίσαο or Δαϊτίσαο, 58, *Lamaka*; Θέστγας?, 119, *Golgoi*; Δαγαφᾶς, 31, 32 (= Δαϊφᾶς?), δογᾶι, 41, *Kúklia*; θέγας, 94, *Golgoi*; before η in φύγη, 126. And yet despite its fondness for α, *yod* not infrequently disappears before that sound even in those parts of Cyprus where it is commonly written.

The period of accurate distinction between the spirants ι̣ and υ̣ in Cyprian is that of the Persian supremacy over Cyprus. Later on, during the rule of Alexander's successors, the greatest confusion pre- vails, *e.g.* Πρώτιϝος, Τιμοχάριϝος, Κυπροκράτιϝος, ἰερέγιγαν, βασιλῆϝος, ϝώρω = Ὥρω, Διγαίθεμι, and Διϝείθεμις.

σι for τι in σί βόλε· τί θέλεις Κύπριοι, and in κέ σις, 60 $_{10, 23}$ (nom. masc. σί τε for σίς τε, 126, is not certain). Cf. also ὅπισίς κε (= ὅστις ἄν), 60 $_{29}$, where τ = σ between vowels. In the accus. neuter τι, 68 $_3$ (after a consonant), assibilation does not take place. Cyprian σίς is

---

[1] Ἀλα(μ)πριγδᾱι, Ἀμηνίγα, ἀνοσίγα, Ϝέπιγα, ἰερέγιγαν, ἰγᾶσθαι, ἰγατῆραν, Μα- λανίγαι, πεδίγαι, τέρχνιγα (thrice), πτόλιγι.

[2] ἀ(ν)δριγά(ν)ταν, Μιλκιγάθωνος.

[3] Διϝείθεμις is interesting; but cf. Διγαίθεμι.

the only exception in Greek to the law that initial τ does not suffer assibilation. Arcadian, Aeolic, and those dialects that change τ to σ, change only that τ which is the Hellenic representative of Indo-European *t.* Cyprian σίς contains τ = I.E. *q.* But the exception as regards the initial τ never becoming σ is an apparent exception merely, since σίς is an enclitic. The interrogative σί is to be explained by analogy to σις.

NOTE. — On πότι, vocative of *πότις = πόσις, see p. 68, where mention is made of an explanation that it is an unfortunate attempt to give a supposed epic coloring to Cypr. πόσις.

σ is frequently omitted in the genitive τᾶ ϝανάσ(σ)ας, and also in the nominative 'Ονασίωρο, 75. Meister's treatment (I, p. 160) of the subject in Boeotian and other dialects is inadequate.

κάτ(ι) κάς and κά, "and." κάς occurs before both vowels (eight times) and consonants (sixteen times). κά is less frequent, once before vowels, thrice before consonants. κάτι in κατ' 'Ηδαλίων, 59 (the only occurrence) seems at first sight to be the progenitor of κάς and κά as well as of καί. καί cannot, however, despite Deecke, B. B., VI, 79, be explained from κάτι. It is rather the equivalent of old Bulg. *čě < qai̯.*

On πτόλεμος, see p. 71.

III. Declension of substantives.

Gen. sing. O declension ends in -ω-ν. Φιλοκύπρων, 60 $_1$; 'Ονασικύπρων, 60 $_{2-3, 11, 30}$; 'Ονασίλων, 60 $_{24}$; ἀργύρων, 60 $_{17, 25-28}$; ταλά(ν)των, 60 $_7$; ὑχήρων, 60 $_{5,15}$; Δρυμίων, 60 $_{19}$; Θεοτίμων, 42 (Apollon); Ἀβιδμίλκων, 59; πε(μ)φαμέρων, 59. With the exception of Θεοτίμων and 'Οναίων, 21 (Berl. Philol. Wochensch., 1886, p. 1292), all the examples are from Dali. Dalian inscriptions also have -ω (ἀργύρω, 60 $_6$, etc.).

Cyprian possesses the oldest historical form of the genitive of -ηυ stems, viz. βασιλῆϝος, 39, 46, 47, 59, 60,[1] etc. But beside the digammated forms we have βασιλῆος or βασιλέος,[2] both of which forms are Homeric. Aeolic, Ionic, Attic, Thessalian, and Boeotian have -ηος, though Ionic, Aeolic, and Boeotian have also -εος. Εὐϝα(ν)θῆϝος ?, 161, Εὐϝά(ν)θεος, 162, as if from Εὐϝάνθευς, which does not occur. Εὐϝάνθη[ς], 163. This form, together with the doubtful gen. in -ῆϝος, may furnish another example of the close interrelationship between the -ες, -ηυ, and -η stems. Cf. p. 78. In the nom. pl. Κετιέϝες, 60, or -ηϝες, if Wackernagel (K. Z., XXIV, 295) is correct in explain-

---

[1] Deecke writes βασιλέϝος incorrectly.   [2] Cf. also ἱερῆϝος and ἱερέος.

ing this termination from -ειϝ + ες. Johansson has, however, vig-orously disputed the correctness of Wackernagel's reasoning. See especially Chapter II of his De derivatis verbis contractis.

Declension of -κλῆς. The full form of the nominative appears in Νικοκλέϝης, 40, gen. Νικοκλέϝος, 179 ; Θεοκλέος, 126 ; Τιμοκλέος, 35 ; but Τιμοκλέϝεος, 36, 64. In Arcadian I find eighteen different names with the nom. in -κλῆς, and no instance of -κλέϝης or -κλέης ; in the genitive, -κλέος in fourteen different names. The Arcadian inflec-tion is younger than the Cyprian. Of the two genitive forms in Cyprian, Νικοκλέϝος is not so original as Τιμοκλέϝεος ; cf. Boeot. κλειος < κλεεος. There is no trace of -κλη in the genitive as in Aeolic (Θεόκλη, 288), or of the Attic and Delphic -κλέου.

IV. Pronominal declension.

μι for με in No. 2[1]; cf. μεν in 71, μιν in 45, by Voigt and Hall's corrections.

V. Conjugation.

ἔκερσε, 31, 32 ; see pp. 92, 106.

ἐπισταῖς in 68 = ἐπισταίης, from the analogy of plural forms by a process which is the opposite to that which produced the Herodo-tean and later Attic δοίημεν ἐνθείητε, etc. The form stands alone, I believe.

ἐλθετῶς · ἀντὶ τοῦ ἐλθέ. Σαλαμίνιοι. cf. δίδως, etc.

δοϝεναι (accent uncertain) is the earliest form of this infinitive. -ναι seems to have been crowded out in all other dialects except Ionic-Attic. δόμε(ν), 126, is a Homeric reminiscence, as ἐνιπή.

VI. Prepositions, Particles.

A preposition ὐ with the primary signification of "up" occurs in Cyprian ὔχηρος, *extra pay,* Ὑϝέλθων[2] = Ἀναβαίνων,[3] ὔϝ-αις ζᾶν, 60 10, 22-23, 28, *for life.* In the latter case the sense is not far different from ἀνὰ χρόνον, ὐ ϝαρον, *to the festival;* ὐ τύχα[ι], 74 3 = ἐπὶ τύχη = ἐν τύχῃ. Its occurrence in Pamphylian and in Carian is very doubtful.

---

[1] In No. 1, Voigt thinks με is preferable to μι, since the character closely re-sembles that of 15. Hall, however, reads μι, which may be either (epigraphi-cally) dialectic for με or for μι(ν), as in 45.

[2] This name, together with Εὐϝέλθων, 123, 171, etc., is remarkable as being entirely new, there being but few, if any, others with -ελθων as a final member. In the coining of a new proper name it is necessary that the initial or final mem-ber should have already been in use; cf. Εὐϝαγόρας, etc.

[3] An earlier name of the Maeander.

Pamph. Ὑδραμούαν, 1264, would then have to be divided Ὑ-δραμ-.
Carian Ὕβανδα, cf. Ἀλάβανδα, and B. B., X, 191. In ὐευξάμενος, written by Deecke ὐευξάμενος, the ὐ is supposed by Meyer, Gramm.[2]
§ 239, to represent vocalized ϝ. It is, however, difficult to account
for the presence of the labial spirant here. See Brugmann, Gramm.,
p. 117, and especially Baunack's Studien, I, 16, where the subject of
ὐ is discussed, and a weakened force of ὐ (= Skt. *ud*) assumed in
ὐευξάμενος. Hall, Rev. A. O. S., XI, 216, settles the difficulty by reading μι(ν) εὐξάμενος.

The Cyprian dialect is peculiar in possessing certain particles not
found elsewhere. These are ἰδέ, νυ, and παι. The use of δέ, though
frequent in Arcadian, is entirely foreign to the Cyprian idiom. Its
place is taken by ἰδέ, *and*, for which ἰ appears in 60₂₄. But ἰδέ is
used with the force of δέ in apodosis. This ἰδέ suggests the Sanskrit
id, and may perhaps serve to explain δέ in such connection as ὁ δέ,
which is hardly ὁ + δέ.

-νυ for -νε is read by Sayce on the inscription from Tamassus (Berl.
Phil. Wochens., 1886, p. 1323). The enclitic νυ, 60₆,₁₆. Cf. A. J. P.,
VIII, 471.

The particle παι appears in κάς παι, 60₄; ἰδέ παι, 60₁₂; τάς παι, 71.
Whether we are to write παι or πᾳ is not certain. If παι, we may
then compare αἰ (cf. above, p. 72), locative from the stem *svā*. πῇ
πήποκα ὅπη then contain the instrumental of πο-. If πᾳ, cf. ὅπᾱι κα,
C. I. G. 2483 ₂₂.

The results which seem to me justified by an examination
of the phonology and inflection of Arcadian and Cyprian are
as follows : —

I. *Nature of the connection between Arcadian and Cyprian.* —
Arcadian and Cyprian are in closer touch than any other two
Hellenic dialects, which have at the same time so many and
such varied points of divergence. If we consider the date of
the separation of the daughter dialect (a date which on any
view must be early, even if we reject the legend handed down
by Pausanias), the preservation in Arcadian and Cyprian for
so many centuries of autonomous existence of so many cases
of agreement in form and in syntactical usage, affords a most
striking example of the conservative force of dialect life.
This resistance to external influence was effected, it must
be remembered, to no inconsiderable extent on the lines of a

syntactical usage which must have encountered the det:r-
mined hostility of common speech (ἐσς with the gen., ἀπύ
with the dat.).   This pertinacity of linguistic tradition in
Arcado-Cyprian is more marked than that displayed by
either Aeolic, or Thessalian, or Boeotian, dialects which offered no such stubborn resistance to the elements of disin-
tegration, and which not unwillingly adopted forms alien
to the genius of the speech of that territory in North-eastern
Hellas, whence they all sprang.

II. *Connection of Arcado-Cyprian with Aeolic, Thessalian,
Boeotian, and Elean.* — There is no single striking dialectic
feature possessed in common by Arcado-Cyprian, Aeolic,
Thessalian, Boeotian, and Elean.   It might indeed seem that
in the retention of the I.E. pronunciation of υ, these dialects
had a meeting-ground.   But the Thessalian and Aeolic pronunciation of υ is not certain ; and even if it were *u* and not
ü, the retention of a pan-Hellenic sound is no proof of any
closer bond, unless it can be shown that before the division
into dialects, the other Greeks had adopted the later sound
ü, while the Arcadians, Aeolians, etc., living in closer geographical unity, alone clung to their *u*.   This cannot, however, have been the case, since the Spartans, too, retained
with tenacity the older pronunciation.   And again, it might
seem possible that the preservation of the strong form ερ was
a distinguishing feature of all these dialects.   In Cyprian, it
is true, we have no instance of θέρσος, though we have
Ἀριστοκρέτης ; but no single word maintains the strong form
throughout the six dialects in question.   It is doubtless
undeniable that Doric has few, if any, cases of ερ for αρ or
ρα ; but the co-existence of both strong and weak forms as
early as Homer indicates that we must not be hasty in
ascribing the ερ forms to all the subdivisions of a single
" Aeolic " dialect, though it is clear that there obtains a
tendency in all these dialects to favor the retention of the
older of the two pre-dialectic forms ερ and αρ (ρα).

Whenever we start with a phonetic change that might
seem adapted to serve as a criterion, the line of argument is
uniformly broken.   Thus if we start with ἀπύ, or κέ, Boeo-

tian and Elean are the offending dialects; if with ἐσς or with ἐν *cum accus.*, Aeolic is the guilty member.

In fact, every argument that has been adduced, from the point of view of language, in favor of a pan-Aeolic dialect, fails to hold ground. Labialism (for the dentalism of the other dialects) is clearly not a phase of "Aeolic" phonetic life.

The universality of assibilation can only be upheld by assuming that ντι had not become νσι in the ground Aeolic, but νθι, the θ of which is held to represent a sound between τ and σ. The dulling of closed *o* to *υ* may be pan-Aeolic, but only in a few words.

Aeolic is bound to Thessalian and to Boeotian by close ties, Thessalian to Boeotian, and Arcadian and Cyprian to Aeolic, Thessalian, and Boeotian by a series of certain and oftentimes unique links, and each is connected with the other by a series of minute correspondences. Aeolic, Thessalian, and Boeotian are more closely connected than any other dialects of this class; yet they have only one salient feature in common. If we extend our horizon to embrace Arcado-Cyprian and Elean, the attempt to apply the same arguments and gain the results that have accrued to us by an investigation of Doric or of Ionic, is shattered by the logic of unyielding facts. Curtius pronounced long ago in favor of an Aeolic dialect embracing all the sub-dialects except perhaps Elean. Gelbke followed with a more positive assertion, but based on fewer facts. Kirchhoff restricted Aeolic to the dialect of Lesbos and denominated Thessalian and Boeotian Doric. But one who is apparently his scholar, Brand, has now sought to become a unitarian of the unitarians. He is not content with assuming cases of dialect agreement; he ventures upon the dangerous essay of explaining away all cases of divergence. It is true that certain recent researches have taken a position in favor of an early influence of Ionic which has heretofore not been accorded it. Dialect mixture should, I think, have room and verge enough; but when recourse is had to it, it must be shown in each individual instance that a distinct probability, not merely a possibility, speaks in favor of its operation. If there is to be method in dialectology, it must first do away with such work as that of Brand, who attributes an importance to dialect mixture that was unknown before, and solely because the facts do not fit in with his theory.   Gerrymandering dialect phenomena cannot but hurt a domain of philology that is sadly in lack of material with which to operate.   If, then, there was an "Aeolic" unity, it must have been before the worshippers of the Arcadian Zeus emigrated from Northern Hellas.   Into that period of obscurity it is futile to penetrate with the feeble light afforded us by historic times.   A pan-Aeolic dialect has not been proved by linguistic evidence — perhaps never can be proved.   If it existed, it has left greater divergences in its descendant dialects than either Doric or Ionic.

III. *Arcado-Cyprian in its Relation to Aeolic, Thessalian, Boeotian.* — If we eliminate from the joint possessions of Arcadian and Cyprian those forms that are due to the declining vitality of the old inflectional system, the residue can be claimed as an heirloom from the Arcado-Cyprian period. This is, to be sure, not certain, for many features may have arisen after the separation, and may be of such extreme antiquity that we cannot distinguish them from still older forms such as those which are the exclusive possession of both dialects.   Now, though we refused to admit that any pan-Aeolic dialect had been demonstrated, it is possible that the Arcado-Cyprian dialect may show stronger affiliations to the dialects akin to Aeolic than to any other.   The evidence, above collected, speaks with no uncertain voice in favor of such a connection with the "Aeolic" dialects; and the legend of the expulsion of the Achaeans, an Aeolic race according to Strabo, might even predispose one in favor of an Aeolic connection.

It is a noteworthy fact that the northernmost of these dialects, that of Thessaly, from which, according to the legendary history of Greece departed Lesbic-Aeolians and Boeotians, is the connecting link between Lesbo-Aeolic and Arcado-Cyprian, and between Boeotian and Arcado-Cyprian. See Collitz, Verwantschaftsverhältnisse der gr. Dial, p. 9 ff.

In the Berliner Phil. Wochenschr., 1886, p. 1324, Deecke

has raised the question whether the colonization of Cyprus
from Tegea may not have been an Achaean colonization.
The Tegeans, then, in crossing Laconia to the sea may have
been accompanied by Laconian Achaeans who yielded to the
irruption of the Dorians.[1] Deecke ascribes to a similarity
between Arcadian and Achaean the strong interest in the
development of the Homeric epos claimed by Cyprus (A. J. P.,
VIII, 467 and 481). The worship of Apollo Amyclaeos and
Apollo Helotas points to a prehistoric connection between
Achaean Sparta and Cyprus. Collitz, Verwantschaftsverh., p.
14, claims that the Laconian Ποοίδάν is borrowed either from
Arcadian or from a closely related dialect. Ποσοιδάν may
have been the Achaean form.

IV. *Arcado-Cyprian and Doric-Ionic.* — Where both Doric
and Ionic fall into line with Arcado-Cyprian, the phenomena
in question appear to be survivals of the pan-Hellenic period.

V. *Arcado-Cyprian and Doric.* — Traces of the connection
of Arcado-Cyprian with Doric alone are far to seek; η by
compensatory lengthening (but not ω) has been explained by
the adherents of an Aeolic origin of Arcadian as a proof that
the ancestors of the Arcado-Cyprians emigrated from a cen-
tral point in Northern Greece before ẹ̄ became ẹ̄. But it
cannot be shown that ει for η was a property of Lesbians,
Thessalians, and Boeotians, even on the assumption that they
originally inhabited in common a limited geographical area.
Is, then, the η of φθήρων due to Doric influence, or can it
by any means be shown to be pan-Hellenic? That the
former is the only possible explanation is clear, from the fact
that the ground-form *φθεριω became φθήρω in no dialect
except Doric. An Ionic φθήρω cannot be shown to have ever
existed (despite G. Meyer, § 68). -ερι- in Ionic may have produced closed ε + ρ at the very birth of the Ionic dialect. It
must therefore be confessed that an unbiassed examination
of the evidence makes for the belief that Arcado-Cyprian was
either a Doric dialect, or that it borrowed a specifically Doric
form in a prehistoric period of its existence. Of the two
possibilities, the latter is the more probable from the weight

---

[1] Ἀχαιομάντεις· οἱ τὴν τῶν θεῶν ἔχοντες ἱερωσύνην ἐν Κύπρῳ, Hesychius.

of other evidence. This is the only certain case where Arcado-Cyprian is certainly Doric in character. If the Cyprian ἔχεν be correct, Arcado-Cyprian may be Doric in having -ν as the termination of the infinitive of thematic verbs. But this is true solely on the view that Ionic ὀφείλεν is spurious. If it is genuine, we are driven to assume a pan-Hellenic ending -ν.

VI. *Arcado-Cyprian and Aeolic connected with Ionic-Attic.* — The repugnance to Doric of Arcado-Cyprian in the earliest phase of its existence is as noticeable, as is, on the other hand, the bond of sympathy with Aeolic, and that of Arcado-Cyprian and Aeolic with Ionic-Attic. Whether this closer touch is the survival of the period when I.E. *ā* had not yet become η in Ionic-Attic, or is due to a later, but prehistoric, interconnection between these two series of dialects, is a question that perhaps will always await solution. But Arcado-Cyprian and Aeolic, despite their divergences, stand out in clearer lines of opposition to Doric than do Thessalian and Boeotian, and on the other hand, seem to form a link in the chain which begins with Doric and ends with Ionic-Attic. This statement must, however, not be forcibly construed to imply that Arcado-Cyprians and Aeolians were the first separatists from a common home.

Arcado-Cyprian then points unmistakably to a connection with the so-called Aeolic dialects. If we now descend lower and seek to discover the affinities of Arcadian and of Cyprian when these dialects diverge, and the causes of this divergence, we enter upon an investigation perhaps the most obscure in the whole domain of Greek dialectology.

VII. *Arcadian as distinguished from Cyprian.* — First the dialect of Arcadia. In no canton of Greece is there greater multiplicity of dialectic phenomena so utterly different in color and texture. Arcadia to a greater degree than Cyprus is a veritable battle-ground of contending dialects. As in the petty island Peparethus, three dialects contend for mastery. Its language is but a reflex of the total absence of political union between its mountainous villages; and even the chief towns were a conglomeration of sometime autonomous demes.

In fact, Arcadia was the least cohesive state in Hellas. It was alone the worship of the gods that brought the Arcadians together in a union which was but temporary.

VIII. The correspondences with Aeolic are insignificant, since, with the exception of δέκοτος, they consist of survivals of pan-Hellenic speech. Nor is the connection with Thessalian stronger, since both agree in preserving νς (though in different functions) and in expelling the ν from the same phonetic group. Where Arcadian and Boeotian meet on parallel lines, their cases of agreement are either pan-Hellenic or Doric. Arcadian, Thessalian, and Boeotian agree in a phonetic change which is Doric as well as Ionic. When we embrace a wider area by adding Aeolic to the list, we encounter but two possible harmonies. Of these, one is probably pan-Hellenic, the other (ερ for αρ ρα in θέρσος) is more properly the possession of dialects of "Aeolic" texture, though not their undisputed possession. It cannot on the whole be affirmed that the "Aeolic" predilections of Arcadian are strongly marked.

Its Ionic proclivities are few in number, but most pronounced. The particle εἰ and the infinitive termination -ναι are as marked Ionisms as exist in the range of dialect peculiarities.

The Doric side of Arcadian stands out in a strong and clear light. It is, however, but a half-truth when Schrader states, that, wherever Arcadian agrees with dialects of the "Aeolic" sympathies, it agrees at the same time with Doric. Importance should be placed upon the negation of this assertion, as also upon the character of many of the Dorisms of Arcadian, which can easily be shown to be survivals of the pan-Hellenic period. But despite all this, the aggression of Dorisms from the time of the separation of Cyprian is clearly ever more and more vigorous.

IX. *Nature of the Arcadian dialect as distinct from Cyprian.* — It is impossible to give any completely satisfactory explanation of the concurrence of "Aeolic," Ionic, and Doric forms in a canton of the configuration and situation of Arcadia. This concurrence is one of the most remarkable phenomena

in Greek dialectology, as the combatant dialects of the date
of our inscriptions seem to have been combatants in a prehistoric period, and in a region to which Attic or Ionic especially, could not, in the ordinary course of dialect life, have
found admission.   It is incredible that the Attic forms found
in the Tegean inscription No. 1222 should have been loan-
forms from Attic in the third century B.C.   The vigor of the
dialect speaks out too impetuously for that.

The Aeolisms of the Greek language are passive, rarely
aggressive (as in Chios : πρήξοισι, δέκων).   Where they exist
in the language of the people they have existed from a period
antedating all historical ken.   They are never a force in dialect mixture, save in literature.   Greek dialectology tells of
their ever-receding force, beaten back by the increasing sway
of other dialects, such as Doric or Attic, which are the dis-
integrating factors of the dialect-life of Hellas.

I can therefore see no stable ground on which to establish
any immediate sympathy of Arcadian with "Aeolic" dialects,
save on the view that the Arcadians were once geographically
nearer the ancient Aeolians.   Tradition deserts us in our
search for an original home of the Arcadians in Northern
Hellas.   They were to the other Greeks and to themselves
αὐτόχθονες.

It was beyond the scope of this paper to open up any discussion of the probability of the view proposed.   Its difficulty
lies not only in the danger that over-zealous investigators
may at once assume a period of "Aeolic" unity, but also in
the necessity of showing how the Cyprian forms, which have
diverged from Arcadian, came into existence.

X. *Ionic and Arcadian as distinct from Cyprian.* — The
Ionic ingredients of Arcadian are perhaps due less to Ionic
settlers in Arcadia at the time of the Dorian invasion, than
to the Ionians of Achaea who had been expelled by the
Southern Achaeans, according to Herodotus.   If the Cynu-
rians were, as Herodotus assumed (VIII, 73), Ionians before
they were Dorized, we have in them a possible, though un-
controllable, source of Arcadian Ionisms.

XI. *Doric and Arcadian as distinct from Cyprian.* — The

Dorisms present less difficulty. They are the natural result of the Doric environment of Arcadia. The states of Arcadia, because of no mutual cohesion, became either allies of Sparta (for example, Tegea, Mantinea, Orchomenos) or sought for other extraneous assistance. The later history of Arcadian is the story of the aggressiveness of the speech of the mistress of the Peloponnesus. With this extension of Dorism the statement of Strabo comports well (VIII, 1, 2, = 333) : —

Οἱ δὲ ἄλλοι (Pelop.) μικτῇ τινι (διαλέκτῳ) ἐχρήσαντο, οἱ μὲν μᾶλλον, οἱ δ' ἧττον αἰολίζοντες · σχεδὸν δ' ἔτι καὶ νῦν (19 A.D.) κατὰ πόλεις ἄλλοι ἄλλως διαλέγονται, δοκοῦσι δὲ δω-. ρίζειν ἅπαντες διὰ τὴν συμβᾶσαν ἐπικράτειαν.

The history of the hill-villages of Arcadia or of the rivalries of Tegea and Mantinea, while it explains the possibility of a tenacious hold of ancient dialect-life, at the same time shows that when Spartan influence became supreme, many of the ancient dialect forms would disappear. At the time of Thucydides, Sparta held two-fifths of the Peloponnesus. Even the northern boundary of Sparta consisted of petty Arcadian townships. We have had occasion to admit that even in Arcado-Cyprian times, Doric influence had forced a footing into a dialect that was otherwise in closer touch with "Aeolic." Legendary history but confirms the evidence of language. Charilaus took Aegys ; Oenus and Carystus were Spartan as early as the times of Alcman ; the Sciritis district had been conquered by 600 B.C. ; and though Tegea retained her autonomy, she was under the military dominion of her more warlike neighbor. It was not until the foundation of Megalopolis that Spartan supremacy lost any of its power. But even from the battle of Leuctra on, the very memory of that supremacy could not fail to make itself felt in the domain of language which was subject to the control of no Epaminondas.

XII. *Cyprian as distinguished from Arcadian.* —The traces of sympathy between Cyprian and Aeolic, or Thessalian, or Boeotian, are not strongly marked. With Aeolic Cyprian has κυμερ- for κυβερ-, but its other points of agreement with Aeolic and the other dialects of this class are generally shared in by either Ionic or Doric. The connection of Arcadian with

Aeolic is perhaps stronger than that of Cyprian with Aeolic. Cyprian, Aeolic, Thessalian, and Boeotian have resisted longer than Doric the ingression of the Ionic ν ἐφελκυστικόν.

With Doric, Cyprian, apart from Arcadian, seems in closer touch than with Ionic ; which need not be wondered at, since Rhodes, Crete, Pamphylia, and other settlements of Doric growth were not far distant. Curium is said to have been settled by an Argive colony (Strabo, XIV, 683 ; Hdt. V, 113) ; and one of the neighboring towns was called Argos.

XIII. *Character of the differences between Arcadian and Cyprian.* — If we compare those cases in which there is an absolute disagreement between Arcadian and Cyprian, it is evident that either the one dialect or the other has preserved the more ancient form. In some instances where it is impossible to fix the chronology of a phonetic change or where two variant forms appear to antedate the separation into dialects, we can obtain no light as to the relative priority of Arcadian or of Cyprian.

Thus Arcadian has τει-, Cyprian πει- (ἀποτειέτω, πείσει), Arcadian πόλις, Cyprian πτόλις, Arcadian εἰ, Cyprian ἤ.

The "acorn-eating" Arcadians are less prone to admit innovations than their offspring. Thus they have preserved antevocalic ε, the ancient locative plural, though in but a single example, -αυ from ᾱ + σιο, instead of adopting, as the Cyprians occasionally have done, the Doric -ᾱ or the Ionic -ω ; in the O declension they have kept the termination pure, refusing to allow the adhesion of ν ; they have not suffered ἄλλων to be softened into αἴλων ; they have resisted the expulsion of secondary intervocalic σ (Cyprian φρονέωι) ; they have preserved σ where it is in place (Cyprian τᾶ ϝανάσ(σ)ας) ; they have not changed τ from I.E. *q* to σ ; they have no ζ for δι- That ἀν = ἀνά is a loan-form in Arcadian, though older than ὀν, is probable, since it is difficult to account for a later ingression of an Aeolic form into Cyprus. The Aeolisms of Cyprus are generally joint possessions of Arcadian and Cyprian. It is more probable that Arcadian should have adopted Dorisms than that Cyprian should have lost Aeolisms.

But as in the offspring hereditary traits are reproduced

which have not appeared in the parent, so Cyprian is oftentimes the representative of a more ancient period than Arcadian. It has the oldest genitive of the ηυ- stems in βασιλῆϝος; it has the ancient -κλέϝεος, whereas the Arcadian genitive is invariably -κλέος; it has ἔκερσε, whereas Arcadian, even on the view that the vexatious φθέραι is for φθήραι, is younger; it has ᾶς in the feminine genitive, while Arcadian has -αυ. And furthermore, it has clung tenaciously to such an older form as -ει in the dative of -ες stems, where Arcadian has πλήθι.

INDEX.

I.

THE ARCADO–CYPRIAN DIALECT. — *ADDENDA.*

In the interval between the completion of my paper on the Arcado-Cyprian dialect and its publication, I have collected the following *addenda.*

Page 61, note. The verb ϝέχω derives additional confirmation from the Cyprian ἴϝεξε (*Studia Nicolaitana*, p. 67). This (ϝ)έχω appears in γαιϝοχος, and is to be distinguished from (σ)έχω.

Page 75, note 3. Read *Eubœan.* On the pronunciation of οι in Styra, see Bechtel, *Inschriften des ion. Dialekts*, pp. 17, 37.

Page 80. The instance of Cretan ἰν *cum accus.* might recall the supposed case of ἐν *cum accus.* in Laconian (ἐλ Λακεδαίμονα, Cauer 26₈). This is however = ἐς Λακ.

Page 92. Brugmann (*Grundriss*, § 131) maintains that ἀμείνων is from ἀμεν-ϳων by compensatory lengthening. Brugmann, as well as Meister, takes no account of the character of the diphthong in Attic inscriptions (ἀμΕΙνων). Brugmann (§ 639), following Osthoff, even goes so far as to refer the genuine ΕΙ of ὀλείζων μείζων to the influence of ἀμείνων, which, on his view, must have a spurious ΕΙ.

Page 95. I now prefer to explain δαμιοργοί as arising from δαμιο(ε)ργοί. There are three methods of treating compounds whose final member is -εργος or -εργης. See Bechtel, *Inschr. des ion. Dial.* p. 190.

A. Non-contraction of the vowels in contact. ὀβριμοεργῶν, Callinus 3; ἀγαθοεργοί, Hdt. A 67, etc.; λυκιοεργέας, Hdt. H 76, cf. A 65 hexam.

B. By contraction of the vowels.

    1. παναλουργέα, Xenoph. 3₅; ὑπουργημάτων, Hdt. A 137. Τηιουργός, μιλησιουργής, χιουργής in the Delian inventory of the temple of Apollo (Dittenb. *Sylloge*, 367); Λυκοῦργος, Styra, 19₁₅.

    2. καρικεϳργέος, Anacr. 91.

C. By expulsion of one of the vowels.

    1. ἀλοργήν, Samos, 220₁₅. ₁₆. ₁₉, and ἀλοργάς, ἀλοργά, ἀλοργοῦς, ἀλοργοῦν, παναλοργές δημιοργοῦ in the same inscription; ἱροργίαι, Hdt. E 83 (in Mss. A B C). Cf. Ὀλόντιοι in Cretan, Ὀπόντιοι in Locrian, Σελινόντιος Coll. Samml. No. 3044.

    2. δημιεργός, Nisyros (Dittenb. *Syll.* 195); λινεργής, Lycoph. 716.

Page 97. The form [ἐλλανο]δικόντοιν should also appear under a separate section (cf. p. 112), illustrating the disappearance of the ε of εο in contract verbs. This phenomenon is foreign to Cyprian, and occurs in Arcadian only in this word. See G. Meyer, Gramm. § 151.

Page 104. Instances of oρ, ρο = αρ, ρο, even in Ionic, show how weak the hold of Aeolic is upon these forms. Βρόταχας, Panticapaion 117, Ephesus (Wood, *Discov. at Eph.* App. 2, no. 2), in Xenophanes, according to the *Et. Mag.*, and in the name of a Gortynian, Simonides Ceos 127, is equivalent to βράταχος = βάτραχος, Germ. *Kröte;* πορδακοῖσιν, Sim. Amorg. 21 = Attic παρδακός. Archil. (140) has παρδοκόν, and Hdt. βάτραχος or βάθρακος.

Page 108. Cf. Cyprian υἰϝεῖ, *Athenæum*, 1882, No. 2847, p. 644.

Page 111. In reference to the Cyprian genitives Εὐϝαγόρω and ’Αμύντω, ascribed by Meyer to Ionic influence, it should be said that in no Ionic inscription, except Halic. 240 B 3, is there a genitive in -αγόρω. We find ’Αμύντεω, Halic. 240₂₆, and ’Αμύντα, Iasos 104₂₁. ₂₄. For the Ionic genitives in -ω of Bechtel, *Inschr. des. ion. Dial.* p. 109.

Page 111. ὤρη, quoted from an inscription from Miletus, has, according to Bechtel (on No. 100), nothing to do with οὐρά, but is = Lat. sūra. Cf. Schol. H. Q. on Od. μ 89.

Page 112. Third line from end, insert before *inter* the word *littera*.

Page 114. On αἶλος, cf. Brugmann, *Grundriss*, § 639.

Page 114. ἄρμυλα α' ὑποδήματα, Κύπριοι and ἄρμωλα· ἀρτύματα,’Αρκάδες do not prove the interchange of ω and υ.

Page 118. The vocative δέσποτε, *Bull. Corr. Hellen.* III. 165, No. 7, 2 is noticeable.

Abbreviations: *Hall. Rev. A. O. S.* = Hall's Review of Deecke's Collection, in the eleventh volume of the Journal of the Amer. Orient. Soc. *G. G. A.* = Göttingener Gelehrte Anzeigen.

H. W. S.

August 1, 1888.

CPSIA information can be obtained
at www.ICGtesting.com
Printed in the USA
BVOW09s2112081117
499880BV00023B/865/P